ECONOMIC COMMISSION FOR EUROPE
Geneva

Water Series No. 3

Protection of Transboundary Waters

Guidance for policy- and decision-making

UNITED NATIONS
New York and Geneva, 1996

NOTE

Symbols of United Nations documents are composed of capital letters combined with figures. Mention of such a symbol indicates a reference to a United Nations document.

*

*   *

The designations employed and the presentation of the material in this publication do not imply the expression of any opinion whatsoever on the part of the Secretariat of the United Nations concerning the legal status of any country, territory, city or area, or of its authorities, or concerning the delimitation of its frontiers or boundaries.

ECE/CEP/11

UNITED NATIONS PUBLICATION
Sales No. E.96.II.E.25 ISBN 92-1-116658-6
ISSN 1020-0886

PREFACE

The economic and environmental relevance of transboundary watercourses and international lakes is clearly demonstrated by their size. In fact, more than 50 per cent of Europe's 31 rivers with a drainage area of over 50,000 km² have transboundary catchments. Moreover, many small and medium-sized waters criss-cross the boundaries between two or more States. The Finnish-Russian inventory of transboundary waters, for example, lists more than 400 transboundary catchment areas, and in the catchment areas of the rivers Rhine and Meuse more than 130 small rivers cross the border with the Netherlands. For decades, transboundary waters in Europe have played an important economic role without particular thought being given to the notion of preventing, controlling and reducing transboundary impact.

In recent decades, the needs and benefits of cooperating on the protection and sustainable use of transboundary waters have gained wide recognition among countries. However, cooperation in regard to various waters was based on differing underlying principles. Significant efforts have therefore been made under the auspices of the United Nations Economic Commission for Europe (ECE) to promote a coordinated regional approach. Intensive negotiations and cooperative action produced agreement on a number of policy declarations and recommendations to governments to respond to the challenges of environmental protection and the sustainable use of resources. These soft-law instruments were at the root of the *Convention on the Protection and Use of Transboundary Watercourses and International Lakes*, which was adopted at Helsinki on 17 March 1992 and enters into force on 6 October 1996.

Numerous examples illustrate the efforts and successes of countries to overcome problems associated with the pollution of transboundary waters. A number of ECE countries have defined national strategies for the protection and use of water resources or are in the course of drawing up new strategies to respond to specific objectives of the Convention. While the strategies vary from country to country, a common thread runs through all of them. There is agreement on the application of the precautionary principle, the polluter-pays principle, and the principle of sustainable water management as the major guiding principles for cooperation on transboundary waters. Many countries have also expressed the need to limit waste-water emissions and to take other comprehensive water-quality measures.

At the same time, countries voiced a need to share experience on other specific measures to cut emissions into transboundary waters and to ensure the conservation, and where necessary, the restoration of ecosystems. Thus, the ECE Working Party on Water Problems, which was entrusted with the interim implementation of the Convention, focused its activities on such issues as the ecosystem approach in water management, the prevention of water pollution from hazardous substances, water-quality criteria and objectives, and the prevention and control of water pollution from fertilizers and pesticides in agriculture. These activities have led to a number of studies, guidelines and recommendations to governments, published in the first and second volumes of the Water Series (ECE/ENVWA/31 and ECE/CEP/10).

Further guidance was needed on three distinct issues: information for decision-making, specific measures to protect groundwaters, and licensing waste-water discharges into transboundary waters. To this end, the Committee on Environmental Policy, at its third session in May 1996, adopted the Guidelines on water-quality monitoring and assessment of transboundary rivers; the Recommendations to ECE Governments on specific measures to prevent, control and reduce groundwater pollution from chemical storage facilities and from waste-disposal sites; and the Guidelines on licensing waste-water discharges from point sources into transboundary waters.

Information for decision-making

Improving the protection of waters and reducing transboundary impact require reliable data and information. There is growing evidence that the availability and reliability of water-quality and water-quantity data in Europe is improving, and progress is being made in the introduction and use of harmonized data collection, reporting and assessment procedures. Examples at the subregional level include activities of joint bodies, such as those established for the Finnish-Russian waters; the rivers Danube (*ad interim*), Elbe, Oder (*ad interim*) and Rhine; the lakes Constance and Geneva; and Italo-Swiss lakes.

For other transboundary catchment areas, however, data availability and reliability are still inadequate and require joint efforts under the Convention to avoid piecemeal solutions. A specific task force on monitoring and assessment, with the Netherlands as lead country, has been established aimed at improving the situation significantly. The output of the first phase of its activities were the *Guidelines on water-quality monitoring and assessment of transboundary rivers*, contained in part I of the present publication. These are based on a thorough examination of current monitoring and assessment practices as referred to in annex I to these Guidelines.

Experts from some twenty countries participated in the task force. Networking with other organizations and institutions which carry out programmes on monitoring and assessment of fresh waters was one of the main aims of the task force to make the best use of their experience and avoid duplication of efforts. Representatives of the World Meteorological Organization's secretariat (WMO), the European Environment Agency and its topic centre on inland waters as well as representatives of the Danube Coordination Unit and of the working groups established under the Environmental Programme for the Danube River Basin also participated in various task force activities.

These Guidelines on water-quality monitoring and assessment of transboundary rivers are intended to assist ECE Governments and joint bodies (e.g. river-basin commissions) in developing and implementing procedures for monitoring and assessing transboundary waters in their regions following the provision of the Convention "to harmonize rules for the setting-up and operation of monitoring programmes, measurement systems, devices, analytical techniques, data processing and evaluation procedures, and methods for the registration of pollutants discharged" (art. 11, para. 4).

The target group comprises decision makers in environmental and water ministries and agencies and all those who are responsible for managing the monitoring and assessment of transboundary rivers. The character of these Guidelines is strategic rather than technical. They refer to transboundary rivers. Step by step, guidelines on the monitoring and assessment of other transboundary water bodies (groundwater, lakes, estuaries) will also be drawn up, and experience will be gained in the implementation of these guidelines in pilot projects, as is now the case with the Guidelines related to transboundary rivers.

The Guidelines emphasize water-quality aspects of the monitoring and assessment of transboundary rivers. Where relevant to the assessment of the water quality and the ecological functioning of the river basin, attention has also been paid to water-quantity aspects. However, a number of problems related to information for decision-making have still to be solved. These include a careful study of information needs for the implementation of water-quantity related aspects of sustainable water management schemes in transboundary waters; the setting-up or improvement of laboratory networks in cooperation with the World Health Organization (WHO), WMO, the European Environment Agency and other organizations and institutions to provide reliable water-quality data under the Convention; and the development of a system of accredited water-testing laboratories under the Convention. The Guidelines will be reviewed after a three-year period on the basis of experience with their implementation in a number of transboundary river basins in the ECE region. The results of this pilot project will also serve to illustrate the implementation of the Guidelines.

Specific measures to protect groundwaters

Groundwater protection is becoming increasingly important in the light of the many serious incidents of contamination resulting from the widespread use of fertilizers and plant-treatment substances, from industrial accidents and malfunctions, from the improper handling of substances that pose a hazard to water quality, from contaminated sites (old dump sites, industrial sites— both abandoned sites left open and those still in use— and military sites); and from diffuse sources, such as airborne pollution transported over large areas, run-off from built-up areas and leaky sewage systems. Therefore, the Convention in its article on prevention, control and reduction calls for additional specific measures to prevent the pollution of groundwaters.

The conventional wisdom that groundwater is the best protected water resource—due to the filtering effects of the subsoil and of the covering layers normally found above groundwater—and that it can be used directly to supply drinking-water, is no longer tenable, at least not in this general form. Groundwater damage is long-term damage. Such damage, as a rule, cannot be immediately detected, since there is a lack of suitable indicators that can be used in inspections. Generally speaking, cleaning up groundwater damage is impossible, or possible only over a long period of time and at great expense. Groundwater protection must be comprehensive, and it must not be limited to water-production areas.

To respond to these challenging issues, an ECE Seminar on the Prevention and Control of Groundwater Pollution from the Storage of Chemicals and from Waste Disposal was held at the invitation of the Government of Spain in Madrid, Spain, from 11 to 15 September 1995.

The Seminar was designed to provide a platform for governmental officials to share their experience with the establishment, operation and monitoring of chemical storage facilities and waste-disposal sites; the proper decommissioning of industrial and military sites; and approaches to the restoration of polluted soils and aquifers with a view to preventing, controlling and reducing groundwater pollution. The challenge was to prepare the ground for joint activities of ECE member countries to promote the convergence of national policies and strategies for the protection and use of groundwaters in the whole region.

Moreover, the Seminar was intended to pave the way for additional specific measures under the Water Convention to protect groundwaters against inputs of hazardous substances from point sources, such as a system of licensing involving a range of restrictions on the production and use of hazardous substances. The Seminar also singled out areas where the Parties of the Convention need to carry out common research.

The Seminar prepared the *Recommendations to ECE Governments on specific measures to prevent, control and reduce groundwater pollution from chemical storage facilities and waste-disposal sites*, contained in part II of the present publication. These Recommendations are based on four reports, which will be issued in document ECE/CEP/31. These reports describe the experience gained and problems still faced when protecting groundwaters against adverse impact from waste-disposal sites, decommissioned industrial areas, former military sites, and the storage of chemicals. The Recommendations are also based on more than 30 country papers and the outcome of an extensive discussion.

Control of emissions from point sources through the licensing of waste-water discharges

The recent examination of approaches to the control of point sources and licensing discharges of waste waters into the sewer systems and receiving waters shows that progress has been achieved in many countries, particularly those with market economies, in the development and application of waste-water treatment and sanitation technology, the establishment of appropriate design standards, and the adoption of restrictive discharge authorization procedures. The total load of effluents has been cut by introducing in-plant measures and modifying production processes. Discharge-oriented control based on technological requirements is applied in a wide variety of industries. For new industrial plants in countries with market economies, the application of best available technology is frequently required to treat waste waters which contain hazardous substances and to achieve maximum pollution prevention together with an optimum degree of safety.

The examination also shows the enormous task that lies ahead if countries, particularly those in transition, are to prevent, control and reduce water pollution from point sources. Most countries in transition suffer the consequences of past developments. Industrial waste waters are frequently discharged into the sewer network or directly into the recipient waters without any proper pre-treatment. Moreover, many municipal treatment plants in countries in transition are only mechanical-biological plants. Treatment plants are often overloaded and improperly operated, and they use inappropriate treatment technologies. The degree to which the load of pollutants is reduced is therefore often smaller than expected.

These countries have reported that improvements can be achieved only over a period of time, that priority decisions have to be taken and stepwise solutions sought. However, a clear-cut approach to solving these problems has still to be found. For example, emission limits have to be set for the discharge of hazardous substances.

There is, however, little experience to assess whether these limits are in fact realistic given their time-frames and the associated costs and other constraints in countries in transition.

A specific task force, with France as lead country, has been established with the aim of providing guidance on licensing to governmental authorities based on the best experience gained in the region. The finalization of work on the *Guidelines on licensing waste-water discharges from point sources into transboundary waters*, contained in part III of the present publication, was its major activity. The Guidelines are based on an analysis of different practices of, and experience gained in, 24 ECE countries, as contained in document ECE/CEP/31. The Guidelines deal with such issues as the licensing process in relation to water management plans, the assessment of the current situation, water-quality objectives and targets to reduce the pollution load, licensing systems and supervision of permits issued, economic instruments and consequences of violation. When drawing up these Guidelines, the close link between licensing activities and the other two activities—the work on the guidelines on monitoring and on specific measures to protect groundwaters—has been taken into account.

*

* *

The present publication contains three soft-law instruments in English. As they are crucial for the further implementation of the Convention, they will be translated into French and Russian. Further substantiations for the groundwater recommendations and the guidelines on licensing are published in document ECE/CEP/31. Following current United Nations regulations, this document will be published in English only.

According to established practice, sole responsibility for this publication rests with the secretariat of the United Nations Economic Commission for Europe.

CONTENTS

Part One

Part Two

Part Three

Part One

GUIDELINES ON WATER-QUALITY MONITORING AND ASSESSMENT OF TRANSBOUNDARY RIVERS

prepared by the task force on monitoring and assessment, with the Netherlands as lead country, and adopted by the Committee on Environmental Policy at its third session in May 1996

I. GENERAL RECOMMENDATIONS

The Convention on the Protection and Use of Transboundary Watercourses and International Lakes (Helsinki, 1992) covers, among other things, the monitoring and assessment of transboundary waters, the assessment of the effectiveness of measures taken to prevent, control and reduce transboundary impact, the exchange of information between riparian countries and public information on the results of water and effluent sampling. According to the Convention, riparian Parties shall also harmonize rules for setting up and operating monitoring programmes, including measurement systems and devices, analytical techniques, data processing and evaluation procedures.

These Guidelines are intended to assist ECE Governments and joint bodies (e.g. river-basin commissions) in developing and implementing procedures for monitoring and assessing transboundary waters in their region.[1] The target group comprises decision makers in environmental and water ministries and agencies and all those who are responsible for managing the monitoring and assessment of transboundary rivers.

The character of these Guidelines is strategic rather than technical.[2] They refer to transboundary rivers. Guidelines on the monitoring and assessment of other types of transboundary waters, such as groundwaters, lakes and estuaries, will be drawn up soon by the ECE task force on monitoring and assessment.[3]

---

[1] In the Guidelines, "region" means a geographical area which covers at least one transboundary catchment, unless otherwise specified (e.g. ECE region).

[2] For technical details, the background reports prepared by the task force and leading international literature and handbooks on operational practices of monitoring and assessment (annex I) should be consulted.

[3] The ECE task force on monitoring and assessment of transboundary waters is led by the Netherlands. To draw up the present Guidelines, the task force was composed of experts designated by the Governments of Austria, Bulgaria, Croatia, Czech Republic, Estonia, Finland, Germany, Hungary, Latvia, Netherlands, Poland, Portugal, Romania, Russian Federation, Slovakia, Slovenia and Ukraine. The ECE secretariat assisted the task force to draw up these Guidelines. A representative of the secretariat of the World Meteorological Organization (WMO) also participated in the activities of the task force.

The water-quality aspects of the monitoring and assessment of transboundary rivers were emphasized. Where relevant to the assessment of the water quality and the ecological functioning of the river basin, attention was also paid to water-quantity aspects.

The Guidelines will be reviewed after a three-year period on the basis of experience with their implementation in a number of transboundary river basins in the ECE region. The results of this pilot project will also serve to illustrate the implementation of the Guidelines.

River-basin management

The Convention fundamentally focuses on the river-basin approach, as the issues of pollution, ecological quality and quantitative aspects of a transboundary water are common to all riparian countries. Targets, programmes and measures should be drawn up jointly. Monitoring and assessment activities to support river-basin management with adequate and reliable information should involve all riparian countries.

Downstream estuarine and marine environment

River systems are considered to include their tidal estuaries with (often dominating) sedimentation problems. Given the intense interaction between rivers and the seas into which they discharge, it is essential to harmonize the approaches to monitoring and assessment with those adopted under the existing sea treaties.

Integrated approach

Adequate understanding of the human uses and the ecological functioning of a river, the main issues (see table 1 and chapter II), and the cause-effect relations between issues and uses indicates principally that a river is more than just water. River quality should therefore be assessed in an integrated manner, based on criteria that include water quality and quantity for different human uses as well as flora and fauna. A systematic analysis and assessment of water quality, flow regimes and water levels, habitats, biological communities, sources and fate of pollutants, as well as mass balance derivations, should be conducted in order to provide reliable information.

Monitoring cycle

The process of monitoring and assessment should principally be seen as a sequence of related activities that starts with the definition of information needs, and ends with the use of the information product. This cycle of activities is shown in figure 1.

Successive activities in this monitoring cycle should be specified and designed based on the required information product as well as the preceding part of the chain. In drawing up programmes for the monitoring and assessment of river basins, riparian countries should jointly consider all stages of the monitoring process.

The evaluation of the information obtained may lead to new or redefined information needs, thus starting a new sequence of activities. In this way, the monitoring process will be improved. This should enhance one of the major objectives of most monitoring programmes, i.e. the accurate identification of long-term trends in river characteristics.

FIGURE 1

The monitoring cycle

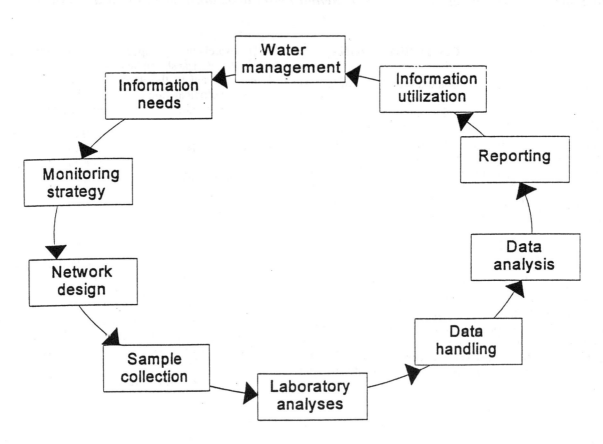

WATER-QUALITY ASSESSMENT:

    Evaluation of the physical, chemical and biological nature of water in relation to natural quality, human effects and intended uses, particularly uses which may affect human health and the health of the aquatic ecosystem itself.

WATER-QUALITY MONITORING:

    The collection of information at set locations and at regular intervals in order to provide the data which may be used to define current conditions, establish trends, etc.

SURVEY:

    A finite duration, intensive programme to measure, evaluate and report the quality of the aquatic environment for a specific purpose.

(According to Chapman, D. (Ed.), 1992. See reference No. 16 in annex I).

Information sources

Information for river-basin management can be obtained from primary sources such as monitoring programmes, computations and predictions with models and knowledge-based systems (expert systems), and other sources (e.g. databases) containing statistical or administrative information (see figure 2). Using these information sources in combination offers optimal conditions for cost-effective monitoring and assessments.

National programmes

The results of national monitoring programmes carried out under the responsibility of national Governments will form the basic information sources under the Convention.

Revision of Guidelines

The subsidiary bodies established by the Meeting of

FIGURE 2

Main sources of information

Water management

Information needs

Monitoring network

Information utilization

Models Knowledge-based systems

Other sources

Structure of the Guidelines

The monitoring cycle (see figure 1) was taken as the basis for structuring the Guidelines. However, the strategic character of the Guidelines implies that much attention was paid to the first steps, including information needs and the strategies of monitoring and assessment (chapters II, III and IV). Network design, sample collection and laboratory analysis will be dealt with in more detail in chapter V on monitoring programmes. For the same reason, data handling, data analysis, reporting and information utilization are combined in chapter VI on data management.

II. IDENTIFICATION OF ISSUES

Water management

The need for information should be based on the core elements in the management of river basins and on the active use of information in the decision-making process. These elements can be defined as the functions/uses of the river, the issues (problems) and pressures (threats), and the impact of measures on the overall functioning of the river basin. The core elements in water management and their interactions are shown in figure 3.

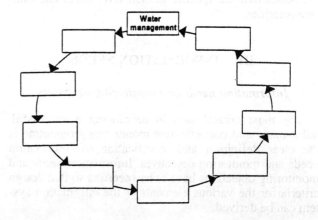

FIGURE 3

Core elements in water management

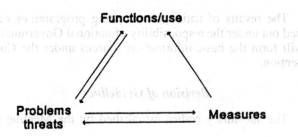

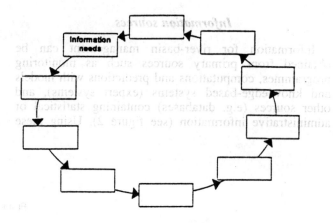

Functions, issues, pressures and targets

Riparian countries need to individually identify and collectively agree upon:

(*a*) Specific human uses and the ecological function of a river basin;

(*b*) The issues which have an impact on human uses and the ecological functioning of the river (see table 1);

(*c*) The existing and future pressures which constitute the issues;

(*d*) The relation between the state of the river basin and the functioning of receiving water bodies (reservoirs, lakes, estuaries, seas);

(*e*) Quantified management targets (e.g. agreed upon water-quality objectives or pollution reduction targets), to be implemented within a specified time period.

This specification of human uses and the ecological functioning of a river and the identification of pressures, issues and targets should include the full range of qualitative and quantitative aspects of river basin management.

River basin specific issues

The issues and targets of water management at different levels (global, ECE regionwide, river-basin level, regional and local levels) should be prioritized, as these priority issues and targets determine to a large extent the information needs. As the Convention focuses on the river-basin approach, riparian countries should identify the issues that are specific to their river basin and indicate priorities.

III. INFORMATION NEEDS

Information needs and monitoring objectives

The most critical step in developing a successful, tailor-made and cost-effective monitoring programme is the clear definition and specification of information needs and monitoring objectives. Information needs and monitoring objectives have to be specified so that design criteria for the various elements of the information system can be derived.

Role of information

Adequate information and public access to the information are necessary preconditions for the implementation and enforcement of the Convention. The ultimate goal of monitoring is to provide information, not only data. As in the past many monitoring programmes have been characterized by the "data rich, but information poor" syndrome, attention should be directed towards the end-product of monitoring, i.e. information.

Information needs per issue

The information required for the assessment of sustainable water uses and ecological functioning should be structured on the basis of issues, pressures and water management measures. The proper identification of information needs principally requires that the concerns and decision-making processes of information users are defined in advance.

Monitoring objectives

Monitoring objectives emerge from the core elements of river-basin management and from the issues that are in the public interest. The main monitoring objectives for both effluents and rivers are:

(*a*) The assessment of the actual status of a river basin by regular testing for compliance with standards. Standards should be defined for various human uses and targets should be established for the ecological functioning of the river basin concerned;

(*b*) Testing for compliance with discharge permits, or for setting levies;

(*c*) Verification of the effectiveness of pollution control strategies, by indicating the degree of implementation of measures, by detecting long-term trends in concentrations and loads, and by demonstrating to what extent the targets were reached;

(*d*) Provision of early warning to protect the intended water uses in the event of accidental pollution;

(*e*) Recognition and understanding of water-quality issues through in-depth investigations by surveys, for example, related to the presence of toxic substances.

The specification of a monitoring objective should principally make clear why the information is needed (e.g. for what decision-making process). It should also

TABLE 1

Functions of river basins and most relevant issues

Functions/Issues	Navigation	Transport [5]	Mineral abstraction	Hydropower	Industrial use	Irrigation	Drinking water	Recreation	Fisheries	Ecosystem	Safety
Flooding	×							×	×	×	×
Scarcity	×			×	×	×				×	
Sedimentation/erosion				×						×	
Quantitative management [1]	×			×	×	×	×			×	×
Salinization						×			×	×	
Acidification [2]									×	×	
Organic pollution [3]					×		×	×	×	×	
Eutrophication			×			×	×	×	×	×	
Pollution with hazardous substances [4]						×	×	×	×	×	

× Main potential pressure or function.

[1] Includes impact of the management of water resources, for instance in the event of water diversion or improper construction and/or operation of hydropower dams.

[2] Dry/wet deposition, eventually followed by leaching to groundwaters or run-off to surface water.

[3] Organic matter and bacteriological pollution by waste-water discharge.

[4] Specific substances e.g. radio-nuclides, heavy metals, pesticides.

[5] Transport of water, ice, sediments and waste water.

Ten basic rules for a successful assessment programme:

1. The objectives must be defined first and the programme adapted to them, and not vice versa (as was often the case for multi-purpose monitoring in the past). Adequate financial support must then be obtained.

2. The type and nature of the water body must be fully understood (most frequently through preliminary surveys), particularly the spatial and temporal variability within the whole water body.

3. The appropriate media (water, particulate matter, biota) must be chosen.

4. The variables, type of samples, sampling frequency and station location must be chosen carefully with respect to the objectives.

5. The field, analytical equipment and laboratory facilities must be selected in relation to the objectives and not vice versa.

6. A complete and operational data treatment scheme must be established.

7. The monitoring of the quality of the aquatic environment must be coupled with the appropriate hydrological monitoring.

8. The analytical quality of data must be regularly checked through internal and external control.

9. The data should be given to decision makers, not merely as a list of variables and their concentrations, but interpreted and assessed by experts with relevant recommendations for management action.

10. The programme must be evaluated periodically, especially if the general situation or any particular influence on the environment is changed, either naturally or by measures taken in the catchment area.

Source: Meybeck *et al.* See reference No. 16 (D. Chapman (Ed.)) in annex I.

---

show the intended use of the information (purpose) and the management concern (e.g. protection of a specific use).

Specification of information needs

Specification of information needs concerns the various aspects of the information product:

(*a*) Criteria for water-quality assessment should be defined. These should lead to the development of a strategy of assessment rather than being a simple inventory of arbitrary needs. The assessment criteria, defined for each use, determine the choice of assessment methodology (e.g. considerations for the setting of standards, or criteria for the choice of alarm conditions for early warning);

(*b*) Appropriate monitoring variables have to be selected. They should sufficiently characterize the pollutant discharge, or represent functions and uses of water bodies, or characterize water-quality issues and/or be of value for testing the effectiveness of measures;

(*c*) Information needs have to be quantified to assess the effectiveness of the information product, making clear what detail is relevant for decision-making. Relevant margins have to be specified for each monitoring variable. A relevant margin is defined as the information margin that the information user is concerned about;

(*d*) Requirements for reporting and presentation of the information product should be specified (e.g. visualization, the degree of aggregation, indices).

Indicators

The use of indicators might facilitate the specification of information needs, since they are quantitative and are linked to certain issues. Furthermore, indicators are often linked to a set of core variables, thereby directing the monitoring strategy for a certain issue.

Evolving information needs and continuity in monitoring

Information needs evolve during monitoring due to developments in water management, attaining of targets or changing policies. Consequently, monitoring strategies often need to be adjusted over time. Dynamic information needs require a regular rethinking (revision) of the information strategy in order to update the concept. However, one should not neglect the need for continuity in time series of measurements. This continuity is necessary to detect significant and reliable trends in river basin characteristics.

Acknowledged general targets

As the Convention acknowledges general targets, e.g. the prevention, control and reduction of pollution loads, a "core set" of variables per issue could be selected for the assessment of the status of transboundary rivers in ECE countries.

> ### Good or bad water quality
>
> A particular concentration of some chemical dissolved in water may reflect either good or bad quality water depending on the intended water use. For example, a concentration of 2 parts per million boron in a river may not affect any present uses of the river, and the river water might be considered to be of good quality. However, if the water is subsequently required for regular irrigation of certain horticultural crops the boron concentration will be too high and the water may then be considered to be of poor quality (that will certainly be the irrigator's view).
>
> (According to G. B. McBride, 1986. See reference No. 20 in annex I. For further information see: Water-quality criteria and objectives. In: *Protection of Water Resources and Aquatic Ecosystems.* ECE/ENVWA/31. United Nations. New York, 1993).

IV. STRATEGIES FOR MONITORING AND ASSESSMENT

A. General strategies

Introduction

After the specification of the information needs, strategies are required to design and operate monitoring programmes in such a way that the desired information is obtained. Strategies define the approach and the criteria needed for a proper design of the monitoring programme. Thus they imply the translation of information needs into monitoring networks.

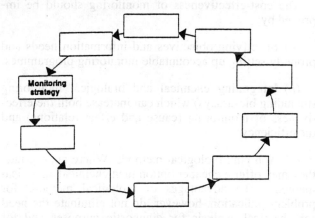

After the general remarks in this section, three categories are considered in more detail. These are ambient monitoring of rivers, early warning and effluents. The ambient monitoring of rivers is further subdivided to provide recommendations regarding the assessment of the ecological functioning, water-quality assessment for human uses, and water-quantity aspects.

Quality of effluent discharges and receiving water bodies

There is a lack of knowledge on actual concentrations of many chemicals due to a lack of analytical methods and/or the prohibitive costs of sampling and analyses. This makes a monitoring approach based solely on ambient water quality inadequate. For this reason, the authorization of discharges of hazardous substances is a basic tool for risk management in water pollution control. Besides, the feedback obtained from the monitoring of the affected surface water has to be used to rationalize and correct the approach.

Integrated assessment by a triad of approaches

The policy used in water pollution control for the prediction, detection and control of waste loads to the receiving river basin, the assessment of the water quality of river basins, and the ecological functioning of the aquatic ecosystems requires the integration of three categories of monitoring:

(*a*) Physico-chemical analysis of water, suspended matter, sediments and organisms;

(*b*) Ecotoxicological assessments by bio-assays and biological early-warning methods;

(*c*) Biological surveys.

The combined use of biological surveys, bio-assays and chemical analyses enhances the interpretation possibilities with respect to cause and effect (e.g. media (water/sediment), contaminants and bio-availability). This approach also leads to a more cost-effective strategy for monitoring, compared with an approach dominated by the monitoring of a rapidly increasing number of individual chemicals.

Inventory and preliminary investigation

Inventories and preliminary surveys should be carried out by riparian countries prior to a monitoring effort in their transboundary river basins. These provide information needed to set up the monitoring as effectively and efficiently as possible. Inventories and preliminary surveys include a general screening of all available information relevant to the aspect under consideration, evaluation of site conditions, screening of the occurrence of pollutants or toxic effects by surveys (by tiered approach, see below) and surveys to determine the variability of monitoring variables in time and space.

Tiered approaches

As monitoring environmental quality serves different aims (e.g. to signal, control and predict) and as the information needs vary from broad indications to fine-tuned diagnostic figures, the choice of selected variables and methods used (e.g. ecotoxicological indicators) also depends on them. Step-wise approaches, which, in general, will lead from coarse to fine assessments, are recommended. Each step should be concluded with an evaluation of whether or not the obtained information is sufficient. Such tiered testing strategies can ultimately lead to

---

> **Trends in chemical monitoring**
>
> The European Inventory of Commercial Chemical Substances has identified about 100,000 chemicals. Several thousand of these are expected to occur in river basins. Of these, concentrations of only 30-40 chemicals are regularly monitored in important European aquatic ecosystems.
>
> An increasing interest in monitoring additional chemicals, and at low concentration levels, may be identified, due to:
>
> - The increase in the number of chemicals which have to be considered in effect assessment, permits and monitoring;
>
> - Increasing knowledge on the adverse effects of pollutants in extremely low concentrations on human health and biota;
>
> - The decrease in the concentrations of individual chemicals in the effluent, due to a reduction in pollution by industry and improved waste-water treatment;
>
> - The rapid increase in available chemical and ecotoxicological analytical methods.

a reduction in information needs for further routine monitoring (see figure 4).

Integration of monitoring efforts

The inventoried and specified information needs will probably require different monitoring networks to fulfil the different monitoring objectives. The integration of monitoring activities for reasons of cost-effectiveness in an early stage of the monitoring cycle may cause an over- or undersizing of monitoring networks. Therefore, it is recommended that an information strategy should be developed per monitoring objective or information need. Integration of monitoring efforts may be considered in the implementation phase.

Phased approaches

In general, a phased approach to bringing into operation monitoring efforts, going from broad to fine, and from simple to advanced, is advisable for reasons of cost-effectiveness. Additionally, for developing coun-

tries or countries in transition, prioritization in time is recommended for the introduction of new monitoring strategies, going from labour-intensive to technology-intensive methods. In many cases, the lack of appropriate, consistent and reliable data and the non-existence of an adequate baseline against which progress can be measured make a phased approach realistic.

Cost-effective approaches

The cost-effectiveness of monitoring should be improved by:

(*a*) Specifying objectives and information needs and properly setting up accountable monitoring programmes;

(*b*) Integrating chemical and biological monitoring (including bio-assays) which can increase both the effectiveness of monitoring (cause and effect relations) and the efficiency;

(*c*) Applying biological methods. Where appropriate, they may offer a cheaper option than chemical analytical methods. The advantages of biological methods for problem indication, however, do not eliminate the need for chemical analysis for diagnostic purposes and for tracing back the pollution source;

(*d*) Using mixture toxicity variables and other aggregate variables;

(*e*) Using tiered approaches or step-wise procedures for the screening of water, sediments and biota to gain more information at lower cost.

B. Ambient monitoring of rivers

The monitoring and assessment of transboundary rivers are concerned with the actual status and trends that are relevant to the functions and uses of the river. To provide sufficient information, this involves ecological, physical and chemical monitoring. The ecological monitoring variables include presence and trends in different biological variables as representatives of flora and fauna. Physical variables include characteristics of the flow regime as well as habitat factors, such as the presence of floodplain forests or spawning grounds. The chemical

FIGURE 4

Tiered testing strategies

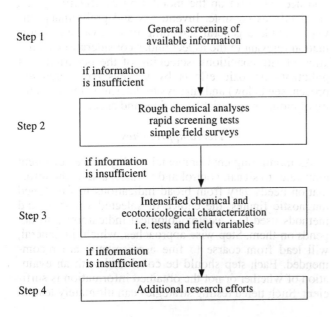

Monitoring strategies

Developing a strategy involves substantial choices:

(a) Is information already available from other sources (models, other data suppliers) or does information have to be gathered by monitoring?

(b) If monitoring is needed, is a general screening sufficient, will a single survey be sufficient or is more extended monitoring necessary?

(c) What types of monitoring are best suited to gathering the data for the specified information need?

HABITAT:

Ecological unit in which the composition and development of communities are determined by abiotic and biotic characteristics, including those resulting from human activities.

RIVER CORRIDOR / RIVER CONTINUUM:

An ecological zonation of communities, both functional and structural, from source to river mouth as a result of longitudinal gradients in abiotic determining factors (e.g. width and depth of the river bed, flow velocity, substrate grain, enrichment by nutrients).

---

variables provide insight into the chemical status of water, suspended solids and sediments.

1. Assessment of ecological functioning

Good ecological quality of river basins

The management of the water environment should at least aim at sustaining or restoring the good ecological quality of river basins where substances or structural components from human activities have no significant detrimental effects on the ecosystem. More ambitious goals such as the conservation and, where possible, restoration of aquatic ecosystems to a target state of high ecological quality should also be considered.[4]

Ecological quality assessment provides a direct measure of the health of ecosystems and is emphasized as a central element in the management of the water environment.

Ecoregions

The functioning of aquatic ecosystems should be considered over catchment areas. Ecoregions (crossing national boundaries) and ecotypes should be fully taken into account. The river continuum (river corridor) concept should be recognized.

Detrimental effects

The aquatic ecosystem may be affected by:

(a) Disturbed habitats and/or the absence of characteristic riverine habitats as a consequence of obstructions/constructions in the river and riverine zone;

---

[4] Guidelines on the ecosystem approach in water management. In: *Water Series No. 1—Protection of Water Resources and Aquatic Ecosystems.* ECE/ENVWA/31. United Nations. New York, 1993.

(b) Emissions of toxic substances;

(c) Organic pollution causing oxygen deficiency;

(d) Nutrient enrichment causing eutrophication;

(e) Human use (like navigation, recreation);

(f) Deposition of airborne pollution (fossil-fuel combustion) causing acidification;

(g) Radioactivity by deposition of airborne pollution (e.g. as a consequence of nuclear accidents) and leakages;

(h) Pollution loads from rivers to receiving water bodies (e.g. reservoirs and seas).

Operational indicators

The quality of aquatic ecosystems is determined by the state of the representative elements mentioned below (see table 2):

(a) Concentrations of dissolved oxygen, biochemical oxygen demand (BOD), total organic carbon (TOC);

(b) Concentrations of hazardous substances in water, sediment and organisms;

(c) Functional variables, e.g. chlorophyll-a, biomass, primary production;

(d) Communities, among others diversity of plankton, macrozoobenthos, vegetation, fish, waterbirds, mammals and, more specifically, the presence of reference species, characteristic of an undisturbed river;

(e) Diseases and morphological deviations in organisms;

(f) Physical factors (flow, obstructions, canalization and meandering, structure of sediments, condition of banks and coastal areas).

TABLE 2

Indicative variables per issue

Issues	Indicative variables	
	Phase 1: core set of indicative variables	Phase 2: additions for extended set
Sanitation	Dissolved oxygen, BOD, faecal coliform, faecal streptococcus	COD, TOC, viruses, salmonella
Salinization	Conductivity	Major ions, Cl⁻
Acidification	Acidity (pH)	Alkalinity
Eutrophication	Dissolved oxygen, nutrients (total nitrogen, total phosphorus), chlorophyll-a	Ammonium, Kjeldahl-nitrogen, nitrate, ortho-phosphate
Pollution with hazardous substances	Floating oil, heavy metals (cadmium, mercury), radioactivity (total α-activity, residual β-activity, tritium), organochlorine pesticides (EOX, AOX), chlorinated hydrocarbons (VOX), acethylcholinesterase inhibition	characteristics of oil other heavy metals of relevance, γ-nuclides (Cs-137), Sr-90, Po-210, endosulphan, γ-HCH, organo-P-esters, atrazine, benzene pentachlorophenol, organotin characteristics of sediments: PAHs (Bornef 6) in sediment and/or biota, PCB (indicator 6) in sediment and/or biota

Selection of assessment tools

Biological assessment tools should be carefully chosen with respect to the intrinsic—actual or potential—ecological value, the designated functional uses of the riverine ecosystem as well as the character and size of the watercourse. The introduction of a reference state provides a standard against which the ecological condition of a system can be assessed.

Biological assessment

The benthic macroinvertebrate community is considered to be a good practical tool for routine assessment of the biological quality of the aquatic zone of rivers. Determination on species level is essential. Assessments include the following indices:

(a) Biotic index: Regional differentiation may be necessary. The establishment of a database of well-defined unaffected reference communities is a prerequisite for the implementation of a biotic index;

(b) Saprobic index: If the organic load is the factor which dominates the water quality, the saprobic index may be used. The purpose of this index is to classify the saprobic state of the running waters, covering the full range from unpolluted to extremely polluted waters.

Integrated ecological assessment

Because of the importance of biotic as well as abiotic factors for the functioning of the ecosystem, integrated ecological assessment methods should be applied. Such methods would be composed of selected "smart" variables (see the above paragraph on operational indicators) that have proven to be representative of a community, and are sensitive to general or specific impacts on riverine ecosystem elements. Depending on the impact, an integrated ecological assessment should comprise:

(a) A biological assessment, i.e. an assessment of the biological status of the river (water body only) with respect to community structure and functioning;

(b) An ecotoxicological assessment, i.e. the application of ecotoxicological tools, such as field experiments and laboratory tests;

(c) An ecological assessment, i.e. an assessment of the interaction of biotic communities with abiotic factors and habitats;

(d) A "whole river" assessment, i.e. the analysis of a river as part of a whole riverine ecosystem with an intrinsic ecological value in which biotic groups such as vegetation, amphibians, water birds and mammals in related compartments such as banks, marshes and floodplains are considered.

Indicative variables

An information need concerning the pressure from organo-phosphorus pesticides may be satisfied with the analysis of the individual pesticides or with the (less expensive) variable acethylcholinesterase inhibition. Both methods would provide the required information. However, costs may differ by a factor of 5 or more.

---

2. Water-quality assessment for human uses

Sustainable water use

Sustained human use of the river basin has to be based on a multi-functional approach in water management. Demands of various uses can be characterized by the specific water-quality requirements (criteria, objectives, targets). Adverse influences of issues and pressures (see table 1) on these water-quality requirements should be identified. This specifies the information that is required for the assessment of water quality for sustained water use.

Indicators and indicative variables

Variables which are indicative of identified issues (see table 2) or human uses should be selected. Aggregate variables should be included, if suitable. Specific chemical variables are included in monitoring programmes if they are the subject of special concern in the river basin (e.g. to test compliance with standards for hazardous substances).

Inventory

A preliminary investigation aims to set up the routine monitoring as effectively and efficiently as possible. Inventories based on in-depth surveys should provide relevant background information with respect to water uses, (possible) presence of pollutants not monitored before, toxicological relevance, variability of pollutants in time and space, and planning of routine chemical monitoring programmes.

Appropriate media

Pollutants may occur in several different media, including water, suspended matter, sediment and organisms. Appropriate media for monitoring variables should be identified considering the following criteria:

(a) Distribution of pollutants over the various media;

(b) Existing objectives and standards (for specific media);

(c) Ability to detect substances (in the various media) within the relevant margin.

Sediment quality

Monitoring of sediment quality is recommended if human and environmental health may be harmed by polluted sediments and when dredging is scheduled. Sediment-quality problems arise especially in sedimentation areas (such as reservoirs, floodplains, harbours, lower river reaches and estuaries) of river basins with substantial pollution and in the event of bank filtration (e.g. for drinking-water production) through polluted sediments. Material which will be dredged should be monitored beforehand. An assessment is needed in order to manage the disposal, storage or reuse in an environmentally safe way.

Identification of hot spots

Hot spots of polluted sediments should be identified through preliminary investigations (inventories). Polluted sediments should be assessed through tiered approaches, using (especially for sediments contaminated with various toxic substances) a combination of chemical, ecotoxicological and biological data.

3. Water-quantity aspects

Water-quality and water-quantity relationship

There is a close relationship between the quality of a water body and its quantitive characteristics. Water-quantity variables influence:

(a) The water quality as such;

(b) The interpretation of water-quality characteristics;

(c) The combined use of water-quantity and water-quality data, for example, for computation of loads, mass balances and early warnings.

Characteristics

The frequent measurement of water-quantity characteristics, such as water levels and river flow, is of the utmost importance for the management of a river basin. These characteristics play an important role for many functions/uses, like water-supply, navigation, ecological functions, protection against flooding, etc.

Forecasting

Water levels and flows should be forecast daily in view of the many functions and uses mentioned before. Especially in the event of high river flows, forecasting is very important. Forecasting is also required during periods of drought when river flows are low and the supply of water is inadequate to satisfy different water uses. As the transit time of accidental pollution in a river mainly depends on the flow characteristics, provision should be made to use hydrological forecasts when accident emergency warnings are prepared for a river basin.

River regulation

The impact of river regulation works and human activities on the hydrological characteristics of a river basin should be evaluated. Changes in water levels, flow characteristics, and sedimentation or erosion may affect the ecological functioning, water-supply, navigation, protection against flooding, and other functions/uses.

Exchange of information

Riparian countries should jointly agree upon the exchange of hydrological and meteorological information and its time-scale (e.g. real-time data in emergency situations; daily, yearly and/or long-term average data). There may also be a need for sharing information on operational control programmes of river regulation works. The agreed upon information should be comprehensive enough to attain the required reliability of hydrological forecasts, water balances, hydrological evaluations and water-quality management.

C. Early warning

Need for early warning

It is recommended that an early-warning system (or accident emergency warning system) should be set up if the direct use of water (e.g. the intake of water from the transboundary river by drinking-water companies) is threatened by accidental pollution and if the concerned use of water can be protected by emergency measures. Measures could include the closure of drinking-water intakes or water management measures, such as directing polluted water by weirs and locks to less vulnerable areas.

An end-of-pipe installation of an automated effluent early-warning system should be used for high-risk industries, if an acute danger of accidental pollution of the river exists and if such a system can prevent the direct threat to river functions by fast corrective action (e.g. to hold up discharges if effluent storage and clean-up facilities are available, or to intervene in industrial processes).

Elements of river-basin early-warning systems

Four elements can be recognized in river-basin early-warning systems: a communicative accident emergency warning system, hazard identification by using a database, the use of an alarm model, and the local screening of river water (early-warning monitoring stations).

Accident emergency warning system

The setting-up of an accident emergency warning system is recommended as a first step in river-basin early warning. This includes:

(a) The establishment of a network of (international) alert centres in the river basin, where emergency messages from national or regional authorities can be received and handled without delay on a 24-hour basis;

(b) Agreements on international alerting procedures;

(c) The availability of a reliable international communication system through which emergency messages are forwarded to the alert centres of riparian countries along the river basin (e.g. the tributaries and the main river).

Hazard identification and alarm model

The following items should be taken up as the next steps when establishing a river-basin early-warning system:

(a) The setting-up of a system of hazard identification, based on a database system for retrieving information on hazardous substances;

(b) The development of a computational model to make fast predictions and forecasts of the propagation of a pollutant plume in the transboundary river or its main tributaries.

Early-warning stations

The initial detection of high concentrations of pollutants or toxic effects at river sites can be performed by regular (e.g. daily) analysis of river water in a nearby laboratory. The establishment of in situ (automatic) measurement equipment in an early-warning station may be feasible if frequent measurements and/or a fast reaction time are required.

Objectives of early-warning stations

The two objectives of an early-warning station also indicate the successive steps in an early-warning system:

(a) To trigger an alarm (accidental pollutants are signalled by regular measurement of biological effects or indicative variables at the monitoring station);

(b) To make a diagnosis for tracing the cause (if pollution is measured or a toxic effect is signalled, water samples taken regularly should be analysed to precisely identify the pollutant using more advanced equipment in a supporting laboratory).

Inventory

Prior to the establishment of an early-warning station, an inventory of potential sources of accidental pollution and available emission data in the upstream river basin (from industries, waste-water treatment, use of pesticides and herbicides in agriculture, etc.) should make clear what accidental pollutants may be expected to occur. A risk analysis should highlight the critical risk factors to functions and uses of the river (substances and critical levels for early warning). Such an inventory should indicate the choice of monitoring variables and measurement systems.

Early-warning variables

Appropriate indicative variables for early warning are specific for each river basin, and should be selected on the basis of:

(a) The dominating pollutants in past emergency situations (frequently occurring local risk substances);

(b) Variables indicative of issues that are specific to the river basin (e.g. dissolved oxygen, pH);

(c) Further needs to detect specific micropollutants (heavy metals, pesticides) using advanced technologies.

The selection of monitoring variables is also determined by the availability of equipment for measurements *in situ* and cost-benefit considerations due to the high investment costs and high operation and maintenance costs for automatic monitoring devices.

Biological early-warning systems

Acute toxic effects can be recognized with the help of biological early-warning systems which use species from different trophic levels and functionality, e.g. fish, water fleas, algae and bacteria.

Effluent early warning

For effluent early-warning systems, the installation of extensive in-plant process control measures (e.g. the installation of safety systems) is often more efficient than end-of-pipe monitoring and alarm systems.

D. Effluents

Policy of prevention, control and reduction

According to the Convention, waste-water discharges have to be licensed by the competent national authorities and authorized discharges should be monitored and controlled in order to protect transboundary waters against pollution from point sources. Limits for discharges of hazardous substances have to be based on the best available technologies. Stricter requirements are imposed when the quality of the receiving water or the ecosystem so requires. In addition, the risk and impact of accidental pollution should be minimized by adequate early-warning procedures.

Objectives of effluent assessment

The objectives of effluent assessment may be identified as:

(*a*) Effluent screening in preparing discharge permits;

(*b*) Supervision of authorized discharge permits (measurement obligations are on the dischargers; they should, for example, carry out self-monitoring);

(*c*) Testing for compliance with discharge limits and the setting of actual effluent charges (inspections by authorities are to be carried out for the purpose of enforcement and control);

(*d*) Estimation of loads, comparison with envisaged pollution reduction or evaluation of remediation activities, getting knowledge on the responses of the receiving water body to the reduced loads;

(*e*) Early warning to indicate malfunctioning or accidental spills in the production process.

Factors affecting the strategy

The strategy in effluent assessment depends on the identified objectives, the characteristics of the discharge (e.g. thermal discharges; oxygen-consuming, saline, toxic substances), the number of discharged substances, the complexity of the mixture discharged and the variability (irregularity) of the discharge.

Inventory

A general screening of the discharge is required prior to discharge licensing. A tiered approach is recommended. The first steps involve an inventory of all available information, followed by a broad chemical analysis and risk assessment screening to determine whether or not the use of further tests is necessary.

Choice of variables

In a pollution charging system, levies will commonly be based on the pollution load. The pollutant load is usually specified by oxygen-consuming substances (COD, BOD) and nutrients. Priority pollutants are not commonly included, though developments are tending towards the inclusion of toxicity to organisms.

In licences for simple discharges, the chemical analysis of specific variables may suffice. In complex mixtures, chemical-specific analyses give only information on the "tip of the iceberg". Thus a large number of toxic compounds remain unidentified. For complex mixtures, whole effluent assessment including toxicity tests may be required in addition to chemical-specific analyses and aggregate variables. Inclusion of these tests in discharge permits is recommended.

Aggregate variables

The analysis of aggregate variables provides an efficient means for rapid pre-screening and may be selected per industrial category. Examples of feasible aggregate variables include organic halogens and acetylcholinesterase inhibition. In general, determinations of organic extractions of water samples (EOX, EOP) should be made (in view of bioavailability) rather than total elemental determinations (AOX).

Whole effluent testing

Whole effluent testing may include tests for the following characteristics: (*a*) acute and chronic toxicity; (*b*) persistence (of toxicity); (*c*) bioaccumulation properties; (*d*) genotoxicity.

Screening for acute aquatic toxicity and mutagenicity forms a first and relatively cheap step in a tiered approach. Current methods for toxicity testing are listed in annex III. The relative investment costs and response and labour time are also given.

Continuous effluent monitoring

Continuous monitoring is recommended for early warning of large pollution discharges or for surveys of short duration to get an insight into the variability of the effluent discharge. Variables for continuous monitoring in effluents may be COD (and other oxygen balance associated variables), total organic carbon (TOC), oil, suspended solids and general variables, depending on priorities and characteristics of the discharge (e.g. specific industries). Recently developed equipment for continuous monitoring of heavy metals, various organic micropollutants and toxicity may be applicable in the future.

V. MONITORING PROGRAMMES

The design and operation of monitoring programmes include many field aspects and many aspects of laboratory work also have to be considered. The design of monitoring networks includes the selection of variables, locations and sampling frequency.

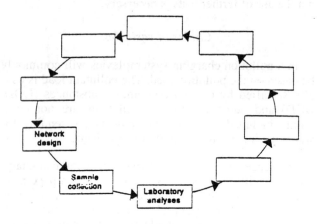

A. General aspects of monitoring programmes

Selection of variables

In general, the selection of monitoring variables is based on their indicative character (for uses/functioning, issues and impacts), their occurrence and their hazardous character. Selected chemical variables should have a demonstrable source or effect manageability. The availability of reliable and affordable analytical methods may restrict the selection of monitoring variables. For efficiency reasons, the number of variables should be restricted to those whose uses are explicitly identified. The surplus value of any additionally selected variable should be subject to cost-effectiveness consideration. Riparian countries should select variables, objectives and standards jointly.

Selection of sites

For the combined use of quantity and quality data (e.g. in case of load computations), the hydrological measurements and water-quality sampling should be carried out, as far as possible, at the same location. If these are different, the relationship between hydrological characteristics of both sites should be clearly understood.

Sampling

A variability over different time and space scales exists for water-quality and sediment-quality characteristics and for biota. The monitoring objectives strongly influence the time-scale of interest (e.g. long-term variations for trend detection, short-term changes for early warning). Therefore, the required frequencies, locations and methods of sampling (e.g. grab sampling, composite sampling) should be determined on the basis of the temporal and spatial variability as well as the monitoring objectives.

Sampling methods

The necessity of integrated versus differentiated water-quality information over time and space should determine the various possible methods of sampling, such as grab sampling, depth integrated grab sampling, time proportional composite sampling and space composite sampling. Protocols to avoid potential risk of contamination should be included in all sampling methods.

Transport and storage

To avoid changes in the quality of samples during transport and storage before analysis, sufficient attention should be paid to conservation and rapid analysis. Conditioning and pre-treatment of samples should follow standardized procedures.

Analytical methods

Analytical methods should be well validated, described and standardized and be sufficiently selective and robust. The required sensitivity, accuracy and precision of analytical methods depend on the defined relevant margins for information use. Standardization is especially important for variables with method-dependent results, such as chemical oxygen demand (COD), biochemical oxygen demand (BOD) and adsorbable organic halogen (AOX). The development and use of analytical techniques with higher performances (e.g. detection limits, accuracy) should be initiated only if defined relevant margins cannot be met, and if this is sufficiently cost-effective.

Inter-laboratory testing and analytical quality control

Inter-laboratory testing should be performed at the national level to ensure that laboratories involved in a monitoring network achieve an acceptable standard of accuracy and precision. To ensure the comparability of data of a transboundary river, inter-laboratory testing on the level of the whole river basin is inevitable. Riparian countries should agree on criteria for equal performance of analytical results rather than on equal analytical methods.

B. Ambient monitoring

Variables

Variables should be indicative of functions and issues of river basins. In table 2, a core set of indicative variables is listed per issue. The selection of hazardous pollutants as monitoring variables depends on:

(a) Noxious, cumulative and persistence characteristics;

(b) Specific problem substances (specific for a river basin);

(c) The probability of occurrence (in practice this should be based on results of, for example, site-specific preliminary surveys).

For specific human uses, standards should be formulated, making monitoring variables explicit. For ecological functioning, variables are specified by the selected method of assessment (indices, habitat factors) and regional reference communities.

Appropriate media

Ambient monitoring should be performed by using the most appropriate media for sampling (water, suspended matter, sediments or biota). The method of pretreatment should also be sufficiently specified (e.g. the need for filtration).

Sampling locations

In general, the selection of sampling sites in a river basin is based on their representativeness for the river reach concerned. The required distance between sampling locations can be critically evaluated from their degree of correlation on the basis of statistical analysis of time series of variables. However, this is possible only if these time series are available.

In transboundary rivers, sampling should preferably be performed at or near to border crossings (e.g. to be able to show the contribution towards reduction targets per country). Sampling downstream of the confluence of main tributaries is important to show the contribution (e.g. pollution load) of different tributaries.

Considerations of the local representativeness of the sampling point at the river site are to be based on preliminary surveys, taking into account the river's hydrology and morphology. In general, locations in the main flow of the river will be chosen. Joint monitoring at the border is recommended to improve cost-effectiveness and comparability of results.

Sampling frequency

The selection of the sampling frequency should be based on:

(a) The variability in concentrations of variables related to relevant margins (in practice based on statistical analysis of time series for variables representative of groups of variables);

(b) The statistical significance and accuracy required for specific objectives (trend detection, load estimation, compliance testing).

C. Early warning

Variables and measurement equipment

Early-warning equipment puts high demands on operation characteristics such as speed of analysis, capability to identify certain chemicals and reliability of operation. Characteristics such as the precision and reproductivity of the analysis are less critical. Pollutants frequently occurring in the river basin in hazardous concentrations should be measured by regular analysis of samples. Simple indicative variables such as dissolved oxygen or pH can be measured by automatic *in situ* sensors. If the detection of specific problematic micropollutants (e.g. pesticides) is needed, advanced analytical systems based on gas chromatography with mass spectrometry (GC-MS), high performance liquid chromatography (HPLC) and others can be used. However, the investment, operation and maintenance costs are high. Toxicological effects on organisms at various trophic levels can be measured with the help of automated biological early-warning systems.

Sampling locations

In early-warning systems, one should have enough time to undertake emergency measures. Thus, the location of an early-warning station should be determined by the relation between response time (the time interval between the moment of sampling and the alarm) and the transit time of the pollution plume in the river from the warning station to the site where the water is used (e.g. water intake for drinking-water production). High river discharges are decisive for the latter. Furthermore, the location should obviously be representative of the intended water use.

Sampling frequencies

The measurement frequency should be determined on the basis of the expected dimensions of pollutant plumes (elapsed time for the plume to pass the station) so that no significant pollutant is missed. A dispersion of the plume occurs between the discharge location and the sampling location due to the discharge characteristics of the river. Furthermore, the frequencies should also allow for sufficient time to take action in the event of a critical situation.

D. Water-quantity monitoring aspects

Frequency

The frequency of measurements and forecasting depends on the variability of the hydrological characteristics and the response time requirements to fulfil the monitoring objective.

Methods of measurement

Many international standards exist for the establishment of measurement stations and for direct and indirect methods for measuring water levels, velocities, flows and sediment transport in rivers (see references No. 14, 15 and 16 in annex I).

Methods of evaluation

Riparian countries should jointly agree on the methods for the joint evaluation of hydrological variables.

E. Effluent monitoring

Variables

The selection of monitoring variables should be based on the actual possibility of the occurrence of specific pollutants in an effluent discharge, based on their application and creation in production processes or their presence in used raw materials. In addition to specific pollutants, increasing emphasis should be placed on aggregate variables and total effluent toxicity testing.

Sampling frequency and sampling method

Sampling frequencies and sampling methods for effluent discharges should be based on the amount and variability of the discharged effluent. Surveys of restricted duration (using continuous or high-frequency sampling) should be performed to gain the required insight into discharge characteristics.

VI. DATA MANAGEMENT

Data produced by water quality monitoring programmes should be validated, archived, and made accessible. It is the actual goal of the monitoring programme to convert data into information that will meet the specified information needs. The main objectives of the monitoring programmes are given in chapter III, and may include the identification of status and trends, the calculation of loads, testing of compliance with standards, early warning and the detection of possible hazards.

Data management steps

To safeguard a valuable, future use of the collected data, four data management steps are required before the data can be properly used:

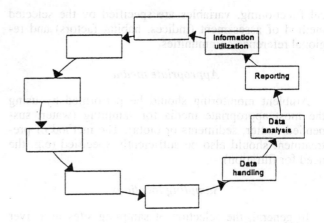

(*a*) Data should be validated or approved before they are made accessible to any user or entered in any data archive;

(*b*) Data should be analysed, interpreted and converted into previously defined forms of information using the appropriate data analysis techniques;

(*c*) Information should be reported to those who need to use it for decision-making, management evaluation or in-depth investigation. The information should also be presented in a tailor-made format for different target groups;

(*d*) Data necessary for future use should be stored, and the data exchange should be facilitated not only at the level of the monitoring body itself, but also at all other appropriate levels (international, ECE regionwide, river-basin level, etc.).

Data storage

Probably the weakest link within the data management chain is the proper storage of data. If data are not accessible and complete with respect to the conditions and qualifiers pertaining to their collection and analysis or properly validated, the data will never be able to satisfy any information need.

Data dictionary

The first archiving of monitoring data generally takes place at the monitoring agency. International cooperation will often involve the exchange of data. To facilitate the international comparability of data, strict and clear agreements should be made on the coding of both data and meta-information. If data are to be stored, more attention should be given to standardized software for data management and data storage formats to improve possibilities for data exchange. Furthermore, framework agreements regarding the availability and distribution of data may facilitate the data exchange. A data dictionary containing this information and agreements on the definition of terms used for the exchange of information or data should be agreed and jointly drawn up.

Data validation

Notwithstanding the quality protocol of analytical procedures, data validation should be an intrinsic part of data handling. Such a regular control of the newly produced data should include the detection of outliers, miss-

ing values and other obvious mistakes (e.g. dissolved concentrations higher than total concentrations). Computer software can help to perform the various control functions, such as correlation analysis and application of limit pairs. However, expert judgement and thorough knowledge of the water systems are indispensable for this validation. After data have been thoroughly checked, and the necessary corrections and additions have been made, the data can be approved and made accessible.

Data storage and meta-information

To be available for future use, data have to be stored in such a manner that they are accessible and complete with respect to all the conditions and qualifiers pertaining to data collection and analysis. Information on the dimensions and appearance should be stored (e.g. phosphate in mg P/l or μg PO_4/l).

Furthermore, a sufficient amount of secondary data (''meta-information''), which is necessary to interpret the data, has to be stored. Characteristics regarding time and place of sampling, type of sample, preconditioning and analytical techniques are commonly stored. If monitoring is performed in media other than the water phase (e.g. suspended solids, biota), relevant meta-information such as total amount of substances in different media, particle size, distribution, etc. should be recorded.

It is essential that any database system is safeguarded against the entering of data without proper meta-information.

Data analysis

Data conversion into information involves data analysis and interpretation. The data analysis should be embedded in a data analysis protocol (DAP) that clearly defines a data analysis strategy and takes into account the specific characteristics of the data concerned, such as missing data, detection limits, censored data, data outliers, non-normality and serial correlation. The adoption of DAPs gives the data-gathering organization or country a certain flexibility in its data analysis procedures, but requires that these procedures should be documented.

In general, data will be stored on computers and the data analysis, mostly a statistical operation, can make use of generic software packages. To ascertain standard automated data analysis, the use of tailor-made software is recommended.

Data interpretation

A DAP should comprise procedures for processing the monitoring data in order to meet the specific needs for data interpretation. These procedures should include accepted methods for data interpretation (e.g. calculations based on individual measurement data or yearly averages, and statistical techniques used to remove non-relevant deterministic influences). Such procedures should also include accepted methods for trend detection, testing for compliance with standards, load calculation and calculation of quality indices.

Data exchange

There is a need for an exchange standard (or format) for the purpose of exchanging digital data. The data dictionary should be the basis for the definition of such a format. Data storage systems of riparian countries should be able to handle the agreed data exchange format. For international data storage purposes, a central system may be considered. This could be a task of a joint body, which includes representatives of national authorities of the concerned riparian countries (see also chapter VIII on institutional aspects).

Reporting protocol

The DAP may be extended to reporting formats for the resulting information. A reporting protocol can help to define the different characteristics for each use or audience and should include certain guidelines regarding frequency of production, information content/detail and presentation format. Monitoring objectives should always be presented as part of the reported information. Standardization of reports is encouraged per catchment

area and/or at the international level (e.g. ECE region). Reliable reports of countries, Parties to the Convention, describing the state of river basins as regards safe human uses and ecological functioning will require improvements in data comparability (i.e. standardization of laboratory analyses), and the development of a DAP.

Reporting

The reporting of information is the final step in the data management programme and links the gathering of information with the information users. To distribute the information, reports should be prepared on a regular basis. The frequency and the level of detail depend on the use of information. Technical staff will need detailed reports more frequently than policy makers.

It is recommended that (annual) status reports per catchment area should be provided to focus on the link between policy measures (societal response) and the status of the water body of concern. A convention-wide reporting which would cover all catchment areas of Parties to the Convention is also recommended (e.g. every three years) to encourage the evaluation of progress made under the Convention, stimulate commitment of the members involved, and make results available to the public.

VII. QUALITY MANAGEMENT

Goals of quality management

The primary goal of quality management in monitoring and assessment can be expressed in the terms "effectiveness" and "efficiency". Effectiveness is the extent to which the information obtained from the monitoring system meets the information need. Efficiency is concerned with obtaining the information at as low a financial and personnel cost as possible.

Traceability, the secondary goal of quality management, is concerned with defining the processes and activities that lead to the information and how the results are achieved. When the processes are known, measures can be taken to improve these processes.

Quality policy

Quality management in monitoring and assessment should be based on the quality policy as declared by the joint body. The quality policy defines the level of quality to be reached. This implies that the joint body should set the prerequisites for the quality management. Quality management can be put into practice only when the management level of responsible monitoring organizations is committed to it.

Quality system

The quality system should document the agreements, in the form of procedures and protocols, of the relevant processes and products, dealing with every element of the monitoring cycle. The quality system should also document the responsibilities with regard to the distinguished procedures. Regular evaluations and, if required, adjustments of the quality system should take place. In drawing up procedures, special emphasis should be laid

---

Quality policy

At the international level, a clear quality policy covering all elements of the monitoring process needs to be formulated. This policy needs to be adopted by all countries involved and has to be elaborated into a quality system. Important elements of a quality policy are a clear description of guidelines, procedures and criteria that all Parties have to adhere to or fulfil, arrangements to control and verify the quality of the information supplied, and a communication programme to ensure adequate flow of information between the organizing body and participants about criteria, procedure, guidelines and difficulties encountered.

(According to W. Confino, 1995. See reference No. 17 (Adriaanse *et al.*) in annex I).

---

on responsibilities at points of decision, such as approval of the monitoring strategy or acceptance of samples at a laboratory.

Protocols

Protocols for sampling, sample transport, sample storage, laboratory analysis, data validation, data storage, data analysis and data presentation should be drawn up and agreed upon by the riparian countries. These protocols are the operational steps in a process where insufficient quality control may lead to unreliable data. By following protocols, mistakes are minimized, and any mistake made can be traced back and undone.

Product requirements

Requirements for all relevant information products should be made explicit and documented. The quality system describes how the requirements are integrated in the processes and how deviations from the requirements are dealt with. Standard requirements on recurrent products are set out in the quality system.

Standardization

Standards should be used for methods and techniques for, among others, sampling, transport and storage of samples, laboratory analysis, data validation, data storage and exchange, calculation methods and statistical methods. Preferably, international standards should be used. Especially in sampling and laboratory analysis, international standards are abundant. If international standards are not available, or, for whatever reason, the use of an international standard is not adequate, national or local standards should be applied, or, if not available, developed.

Standards used in riparian countries should be comparable. Standards used should not necessarily be the same, but for the sake of the exchange of information, the standards used should provide comparable data. The joint body should agree upon the standards to be used by the different riparian countries.

Harmonization

The activities under the joint body should be harmonized. Riparian countries should cooperate when choosing the locations, variables, etc., to avoid duplication and reduce the monitoring effort.

VIII. INSTITUTIONAL ASPECTS

The formulation and implementation of strategies and methodologies for river-basin management largely rely on institutional aspects. These include the organization structures, cooperation structures and responsibilities of involved Parties and experienced staff. In transboundary river-basin management, international cooperation is stimulated by the Convention and is indispensable, although socio-economic differences in the ECE region should be taken into account.

Strategic action plan

Riparian countries should agree on quantified management targets. These targets can be worked out in a strategic action plan for the river basin together with measures aiming at ecologically sound and rational water management, conservation of water resources and environmental protection. The strategic action plan should be based on national programmes and on mutual assistance, and should be confirmed on a ministerial level.

Joint body

According to the Convention, a joint body set up by riparian Parties for one or more transboundary river basin(s) should coordinate the execution of the relevant provisions of the Convention and of the applicable bilateral and/or multilateral agreements. As concerns monitoring and assessment, this includes:

(*a*) The collection, compilation and evaluation of data;

(*b*) The drawing-up of joint monitoring programmes concerning water quality and quantity;

(*c*) The drawing-up of inventories and the exchange of information on pollution sources;

(*d*) The setting of emission limits for waste water and the evaluation of the effectiveness of control programmes;

(*e*) The setting of joint water-quality objectives;

(*f*) The establishment of warning and alarm procedures;

(*g*) The function as a forum for information exchange;

(*h*) The drawing-up of proposals for joint research and development.

The joint body should have an independent secretariat.

Permanent working group

It is useful to establish a technical working group under the joint body which is responsible for ongoing investigations related to monitoring and assessment under the action plan as well as for defining and implementing the monitoring and assessment strategy, including technical, financial and organizational aspects. The monitoring programme should be embedded in the existing national or regional monitoring programmes and should be carried out by national or regional organizations. The working group should coordinate the different programmes.

Quality assurance

To set up, implement and subsequently manage the quality system and carry out the quality assurance, a quality assurance function under the joint body should be implemented. All activities performed under the joint body's programme should be subject to quality assurance and regular inspections of these activities and recommendations for improvement should be made.

Process of cooperation

Procedures for cooperation should be drawn up per river basin in regulations of the joint body. These should include rotation of the chairmanship of the joint body and of the working groups.

It should be further recognized that experience of existing river commissions clearly shows that cooperation between riparian countries has to be based on confidence and needs time to grow. In this respect, a phased approach to cooperation seems most favourable.

National arrangements

At the national level, institutional aspects should be arranged by each country as the lack of these arrangements may considerably hamper international cooperation. Such arrangements include the cooperation between local governments, the coordination of quality and quantity monitoring by various national institutes and the appointment of a national reference laboratory.

Access to information

Riparian countries should mutually provide access to relevant water-quality and water-quantity information. This includes, for example, information on the operation of hydraulic structures in relation to flow forecasting and ice drifts. The public should also have access to relevant information. If progress in water management is made clear, both governments and the public will support measures.

Funding

Riparian countries should provide sufficient funding for the execution of the monitoring and assessment and joint research in the framework of the Convention. This funding should be part of the regular budget. Each country should take care of its own inquiries. Funding can, for example, be based on pollution charges or fees. The establishment of an environmental fund, from which companies can take loans for investments, may accelerate improvements.

ANNEX I

References

The task force drew up background reports on which the Guidelines are based. These include:

1. Volume 1 *Transboundary Rivers and International Lakes.*

2. Volume 2 *Current Practices in Monitoring and Assessment of Rivers and Lakes.*

3. Volume 3 *Biological Assessment Methods for Watercourses.*

4. Volume 4 *Quality Assurance.*

5. Volume 5 *State of the Art in Monitoring and Assessment of Rivers.*

Extensive use was also made of the five volumes and the executive summary of the project "Monitoring Water Quality in the Future". This project was co-funded by the European Commission (EC, DG XI, C5), the Netherlands Ministry of Housing, Spatial Planning and Environment (VROM/DGM-SVS) and the Institute for Inland Water Management and Waste Water Treatment (RIZA) of the Netherlands Ministry of Transport, Public Works and Water Management:

6. Volume 1 *Chemical Monitoring.*

7. Volume 2 *Mixture Toxicity Parameters.*

8. Volume 3 *Biomonitoring.*

9. Volume 4 *Monitoring Strategies for Complex Mixtures.*

10. Volume 5 *Organizational Aspects.*

11. *Executive Summary Monitoring Water Quality in the Future.*

Basic literature on monitoring and assessment was also used. It includes:

12. WHO, 1992. GEMS/WATER *Operational Guide.* Third Edition. GEMS/W.92.1 WHO, UNEP, UNESCO, WMO.

13. WMO, 1994. *Guide to Hydrological Practices.* Fifth edition. WMO-No. 168. Geneva.

14. WMO, 1996. *Technical Regulations.* Volume III, *Hydrology.* WMO-No. 49. Geneva.

15. UN/ECE, 1993. *Guidelines on the ecosystem approach in water management.* ECE/ENVWA/31. New York.

16. Chapman D. (Ed.) (1992). *Water Quality Assessments. A guide to the use of biota, sediments and water in environmental monitoring.* UNESCO, WHO, UNEP.

17. Adriaanse, M., J. van de Kraats, P. G. Stoks and R. C. Ward (Eds.), 1995. *Proceedings, Monitoring Tailor-made, an international workshop on monitoring and assessment in water management. 20-23 September 1994.* Beekbergen, Netherlands.

18. *ISO Standards Handbook 16, 1983. Measurement of Liquid Flow in Open Channels.*

19. *ISO Standards Compendium, 1994. Environment, Water Quality,* Volumes 1, 2, 3. First edition.

Use was also made of publications, such as:

20. G. B. McBride, 1986. *Requirements of a water-quality information system for New Zealand.* In: Lerner, D. (Ed.) *Monitoring to detect changes in water-quality series. Proceedings of a Symposium held during the 2nd Scientific Assembly of the IAHS (Budapest, July 1986).* IAHS Publication No. 157.

ANNEX II

Integrated management of river basins

An integrated approach is a prerequisite to meet information needs for river-basin management in a balanced way. The various aspects of integration in river-basin management are highlighted below.

Multi-functional approach

Various functions and uses of water bodies can be identified from existing policy frameworks, international and regional conventions and strategic action plans for river basins and seas, both for human activities as well as the ecological functioning. The table below presents an example of water-quality requirements set by human uses and ecological functioning.

TABLE 3

Water quality requirements of uses of water resources

Category 1: Uses without quality standards	1. Safety against flooding 2. Navigation (shipping) 3. Transport system (water, ice, sediments, waste water) 4. Mineral extraction (sand, gravel, natural gas, oil) 5. Power generation (hydropower dams)
Category 2: Uses with defined quality standards	6. Process/cooling water in industry 7. Irrigation 8. Fisheries 9. Recreation and tourism 10. Domestic water-supply
Category 3: "Use" with "undisturbed" quality	11. Ecosystem functioning

Uses may compete or even conflict, in particular in situations of scarcity and deteriorating quality. A multi-functional approach tries to find the balance between all desired uses, including the ecosystem functioning. It allows the introduction of a hierarchy in uses and provides the flexibility to be applied at different levels of development of water resources management policies and for prioritization in time. This could be important for those countries where basic needs like supply of healthy drinking-water are so urgent that other uses have lower priority, or for countries where water resources have deteriorated to such an extent that uses with higher requirements can only gradually be restored over a long period of time and in priority order.

Ecosystem approach

Functions and uses of water bodies, issues and pressures, impacts of measures in river basin management and the information needs to manage this complexity are to be viewed in an ecosystem context. Instead of fracturing the environment into manageable parts, the focus should be on the broad "systems" perspective of the behaviour of water in the environment.[5]

A multi-disciplinary approach is a prerequisite because issues and the impact of measures may have physico-chemical, biological, morphological, hydrological and ecological components. The appropriate media which can identify issues and impacts should be considered. It depends on the nature of the issue whether or not information on the liquid phase, suspended matter, sediments, biota is relevant. Interactions of surface waters with groundwaters, air and soil also require an integrated approach. An ecosystem concept is a prerequisite for a full understanding of cause and effect relations within the issues of river-basin management.

Multiple sources

The multiple sources of water pollution require an integrated, balanced, and site-specific approach. If water pollution is dominated by well-defined point sources, monitoring of the discharged effluents may be the best approach. Generally, effluents enter the waters from a great number of point sources, the location of which is not well known. Moreover, diffuse sources form a substantial and growing part of the problem. In addition, the relative contribution of many different sources (agriculture, households, industries, atmospheric deposition) may be relevant to verify the effectiveness of measures.

Integrated approach in water pollution control

Two approaches frequently used in water-pollution control are the emission-based and water-quality based approach. Discharge limits in the emission-based approach are technology-based (the use of best available technology). In this case, monitoring is end-of-pipe oriented. The water-quality based approach starts with the actual or desirable state of the receiving water body (e.g. use of environmental quality standards, water-quality objectives) and may lead to site-specific discharge limits. In this case, monitoring of the receiving water is of the utmost importance.

Both methods have their advantages and disadvantages. A combined approach as followed by the Convention makes optimal use of the advantages of both methods.

---

[5] See footnote 4, p. 9.

Watershed management

Ecosystems do not respect boundaries between local governments or countries. The Convention underlines the need for an integrated watershed approach in river-basin management and adequate monitoring and assessment of transboundary waters.

Institutional collaboration

In many countries, responsibilities for the collection of water information are dispersed over various ministries, executive boards, agencies, etc. Thus, there is a risk of duplication. Often, a lack of coordination may prevent an integrated approach. The establishment of collaborative partnerships and coordination of monitoring efforts of "competing" ministries or institutions may remarkably enhance the quality of the information product and makes better use of available resources.

Annex III

Ecotoxicological indicators and laboratory testing

For pollution with toxic substances, ecotoxicological indicators and laboratory testing by bio-assays can be used for monitoring ambient water, sediment, effluent, and for early warning.

Rules of thumb to be considered when choosing ecotoxicological test methods to assess the quality of environmental samples include:

(*a*) Short-term acute testing is less sensitive than long-term chronic testing. The discriminatory power needed to distinguish differences in time or space is essential;

(*b*) Species having different physiology and feeding strategies will also have a different sensitivity to various pollutants. In general, representatives of algae, crustaceans and fish together can cover a wide variety of chemicals, when concentrations are high enough to elicit responses;

(*c*) Instead of long-term chronic testing, an alternative approach to enhance detection levels is the pre-concentration of environmental samples and a subsequent short-term acute testing. The extraction techniques available, however, will lose some of the chemicals present.

The following freshwater test methods are recommended for use in different monitoring strategies, as they are well described in test protocols:

Effluents

Simple*	Intermediate	Advanced
Toxicity	**Toxicity**	**Toxicity**
Daphnia acute	Daphnia chronic	Zebra fish ELS
Photobacterium (Microtox)	Scenedesmus (algae)	
Brachionus (Toxkit)		
Guppy acute		
Mutagenicity/ carcinogenicity	**Mutagenicity/ carcinogenicity**	
Ames	Notobranchius SCE	
Mutatox		
SOS Chromotest		
Persistence/ biodegradation		
BOD/COD toxicity test following biodegradation procedure		

* Technologically simple, easy to perform, rapid screening, low costs (see table 4 below).

Ambient water

See effluents.

Often the more sensitive chronic test methods (or pre-concentration procedures) are needed to enhance the discriminatory power.

Sediment toxicity

Simple*	Intermediate	Advanced
Chironomous 10 d (whole sediment)	Chironomous 28 d (whole sediment)	Zebra fish ELS (pore water)
Daphnia acute (pore water)	Daphnia chronic (pore water)	Branchiura (whole sediment)
Microtox (pore water)		
Toxkits (pore water)		

Early warning

Simple	Intermediate	Advanced
Artificial substrate with regular sampling	Flow through aquaria with fish	Automatically operating BEWS using fish, daphnias or algae

TABLE 4

**Indication of relative costs of equipment, and the response and labour time
for the above-mentioned bio-assays**

Effluents

	Investment	Response time	Labour time
Daphnia acute	low	low	low
algae	intermediate	intermediate	intermediate
guppy	low	intermediate	low
Microtox	high	low	low
Toxkits	low	low	low
Daphnia chronic	low	high	high
Zebra fish ELS	intermediate	intermediate	high
Ames	intermediate	low	low
Mutatox	high	low	intermediate
SOS Chromotest	high	low	low
Noto-branchius SCE	intermediate	intermediate	high
BOD/COD	low	intermediate	low
toxicity and biodegration	intermediate	high	intermediate

Surface waters

See effluents

Sediments

	Investment	Response time	Labour time
Chironomus acute	low	intermediate	low
Daphnia acute pw	high	low	low
Microtox pw	high	low	low
Toxkits pw	high	low	low
Chironomus chronic	low	high	intermediate
Daphnia pw	high	high	high
Zebra fish ELS pw	high	intermediate	high
Branchiura chronic	low	high	high

pw = pore water

Investments in sediment assessment apply e.g. to centrifuges of high capacity. Daphnia and Chironomus are preferred to Microtox and Toxkits, whenever cause-effect relations are valuable in the assessment strategy (i.e. specificity of response to certain (groups of) chemicals). When only simple screening is of relevance, the latter simple tests are suitable.

Early warning

	Investment	Response time	Labour time
Artificial substrate	low		intermediate
Flow through aquaria	intermediate		intermediate
Automatic early warning	high		intermediate

ANNEX IV

Analytical costs of water-quality variables

Indicative variables

For the indicative variables included in table 2, this annex gives an indication of analytical techniques, investment costs, labour time and operational costs. An extended list of variables gives additional information on some variables which are often applied in inventory studies and for screening purposes.

Water

Parameter	Technique	Investment [1]	Labour time	Operational costs [1]
Dissolved oxygen	electrode	< 5 000 ECU	low	low
conductivity	electrode	< 5 000 ECU	low	low
acidity	electrode	< 5 000 ECU	low	low
Cl	electrode	< 5 000 ECU	low	low
major ions	electrode	< 5 000 ECU	low	low
	ionchrom.	40 000 ECU	intermediate	intermediate
BOD	manual	< 10 000 ECU	intermediate	low
COD	and/or	50 000 ECU	low	low
TOC	automated	50 000 ECU	intermediate	intermediate
Total N	colorimetric	30 000 ECU	low	intermediate
ammonium	or			
Kj-N	titrimetric	30 000 ECU	low	intermediate
nitrate	or			
total P	ionchrom.	40 000 ECU	intermediate	intermediate
ortho-P	methods			
Chlorophyll-a		< 10 000 ECU	intermediate	low
faecal coliform		< 5 000 ECU	intermediate	low
faecal streptoc.		< 5 000 ECU	intermediate	low
salmonella		< 5 000 ECU	intermediate	low
viruses		< 5 000 ECU	high	low
floating oil	visual	...	intermediate	intermediate
oil	IR	50 000 ECU	intermediate	low
AOX	coulometric	75 000 ECU	high	high
EOX	coulometric	no additional	high	high
VOX	coulometric	devices required	high	high
acethylchol. inhibition	colorimetric	40 000 ECU	intermediate	high
organo-Cl-pest.	CG [2]	75 000 ECU	intermediate	high
organo-P-pest.	(GC)	75 000 ECU	intermediate	high
atrazine	(GC)	75 000 ECU	intermediate	high
benzene	(GC)	75 000 ECU	intermediate	high
pentachloro-phenol	(GC)	75 000 ECU	intermediate	high
PAHs	(GC/HPLC)	75 000 ECU	intermediate	high
PCBs	(GC)	75 000 ECU	intermediate	high
Total-α		50 000 ECU	high	intermediate
total-β		50 000 ECU	high	intermediate
tritium		50 000 ECU	high	intermediate
γ-nuclides	γ-counter	high	high	intermediate

Suspended solids

Parameter	Technique	Investment [1]	Labour time	Operational costs [1]
Particle size	piper	< 10 000 ECU	high	low
	part. sizer	60 000 ECU	high	intermediate
organic carbon in per cent	colorimetric	30 000 ECU	low	intermediate

Extension

Indicator

Parameter	Technique	Investment [1]	Labour time	Operational costs [1]
EOP	colorimetric	100 000 ECU	low	intermediate
immunoassays		25 000 ECU	low	high

Screening

Parameter	Technique	Investment [1]	Labour time	Operational costs [1]
	GC-MS: water	150 000 ECU [3]	high	high
	GC-MS. s.s.	150 000 ECU	high	high
	LC-MS	200 000 ECU	high	high
	ICP-MS	200 000 ECU	high	high

[1]   Investment and operational costs are based on west European standards. These costs can differ within the ECE region by a factor of 1 to 10.

[2]   A standard instrumentation should be available to perform routine GC analysis. This instrumentation can be used for different variables, but enough capacity should be available to account for maintenance and method development.

[3]   Minimum standard equipment for laboratories includes GC-MS identification and confirmation. LC-MS and ICP-MS are not to be considered as standard equipment.

s.s.   Suspended sediments.

Part Two

RECOMMENDATIONS TO ECE GOVERNMENTS ON SPECIFIC MEASURES TO PREVENT, CONTROL AND REDUCE GROUNDWATER POLLUTION FROM CHEMICAL STORAGE FACILITIES AND WASTE-DISPOSAL SITES

prepared by the Seminar on the Prevention and Control of Groundwater Pollution from the Storage of Chemicals and from Waste Disposal, held in Madrid, Spain, in 1995, and adopted by the Committee on Environmental Policy at its third session in May 1996

Recognizing the growing importance of protecting groundwater against contamination from industrial accidents, from the improper handling of substances that pose a hazard to water quality, from industrial and military sites, and leaky industrial pipes,

Conscious of the fact that groundwater damage has long-term effects and that existing groundwater damage, with the exception of pollution from sudden accidents, has arisen over long periods of time,

Commending the efforts already made by ECE countries to implement specific measures to prevent, control and reduce groundwater pollution,

Recalling decision E (44) of the Economic Commission for Europe, whereby it adopted the Charter on Groundwater Management,

Taking into account the 1988 Recommendations to ECE Governments on the protection of soil and aquifers against non-point source pollution, drawn up at the 1987 Madrid Seminar on groundwater,

Referring to the specific provisions of the Convention on the Protection and Use of Transboundary Watercourses and International Lakes (Helsinki, 1992) regarding the protection of groundwaters and the restoration of damaged aquatic ecosystems, of the Convention on Environmental Impact Assessment in a Transboundary Context (Espoo, 1991) to carry out environmental impact assessment procedures at an early planning stage for proposed activities likely to have a significant adverse impact on groundwater, and of the Convention on the Transboundary Effects of Industrial Accidents (Helsinki, 1992) to prevent, prepare for, and respond to industrial accidents,

it is recommended that ECE Governments follow the recommendations set forth below:

General

Groundwater protection should be comprehensive, and not be limited to water-production areas. The water quality of unpolluted aquifers should be preserved. While taking into account the distinguishing features of groundwater as compared to surface water, the integrated management of groundwater and surface water should be promoted. The protection strategy should also call for the development and use of techniques to alleviate existing contamination.

To ensure coordinated groundwater policies, efforts should be made, where applicable, to concentrate overall responsibility for groundwater in a single authority.

The planning of new activities which could pollute groundwater should include all necessary preventive measures at the pollution source and containment measures.

The protection of groundwater should not rely on the self-purification capability of aquifers, unless this can be justified by specific local conditions and does not lead to long-term uncertainty or non-sustainability.

Clean-up priority should be given to those sites that threaten legally-protected aquifers and related ecosystems. Despite technical and economic difficulties, the necessary efforts should be made in areas with limited alternative water resources to restore aquifers rather than to abandon them or curtail their use. However, if the aquifer is extensively, severely or irreversibly polluted it may be unreasonable to aim for a complete groundwater clean-up.

Legislation should lay down separate requirements for precautionary and post-care groundwater protection. Precautionary standards are to be used to prevent future impairment. The standards for assessing post care are those established for the prevention of hazards to protected goods and/or resources, especially human health. Using a system of values based on a list of hazardous substances, the authorities have to decide whether or not action should be taken.

Decision-making involves public participation. This requires a public that is informed about environmental matters, including the protection of groundwater. Information should be directed at all levels of society and not merely to those who are already aware of the situation, as is often the case. In particular, efforts should be made to address the younger generation, who are the decision makers of the future.

Prevention

All storage facilities should comply with the precautionary principle. The authorities should be notified of any storage facility for hazardous substances. For facilities with a significant risk potential, official licences should be required.

Storage facilities should be designed, installed, maintained and operated in such a way that there is no danger of groundwater pollution or of any other adverse impact on groundwater resources. Containers should comply with special standards and the type of construction, installation, cleaning and maintenance of the facility and the way it is monitored must be regulated. A licensing procedure should be followed to certify that the construction parts of the facility meet standards. In addition, the construction parts should be installed by specially qualified personnel. The installation firms should set up special quality-control systems.

A twofold safety principle is fundamental. Having two independent safety systems means that the facilities must be situated in an impermeable and stable collection area or that they must be equipped with double walls and mechanisms to warn of leaks.

Authorized experts should examine the storage facilities before these are put into operation, at regular intervals during operation, and after the facilities have been shut down. The operator should monitor the facility to ensure that its safety mechanisms function properly. Particular qualifications are required to monitor and clean the facility. Those carrying out maintenance and cleaning should also be required to set up special quality-control systems.

Landfills should be constructed in such a way that, even in the long term, possible leachate from deposited waste cannot pose a risk to groundwater.

Environmental impact assessment (EIA), hazard rating and technology assessment should be an integral part of the planning, design, construction, operation and maintenance of facilities for the manufacture, processing, storage, recycling and transport of chemicals and waste, as should an analysis of the potential impact of malfunctions and accidents within such systems. Particular attention should be given in EIA to the siting of facilities for the collection, storage and processing of substances and to the movement of pollutants from one part of the environment to another.

To further develop the legal and regulatory framework, efforts should be made at appropriate levels of Government to stimulate research and development on such issues as the distribution of hazardous substances in, and their effects on, groundwater; the movement of these substances between groundwater and surface water; and vulnerability of groundwater. Research and development on effective techniques for the prevention, control and reduction of groundwater pollution should also include methods for assessing damage and mechanisms for compensating for damage.

Assessment for rehabilitation

Polluters, government authorities and the public will accept to pay for the management of contaminated sites only if there is a clearly stated case-by-case assessment, taking into account the endangered receptors and uses. Consequently, instruments to assess and present results should be developed.

A site should be considered to require action only if it poses a hazard to a relevant good/receptor. The hazard should be assessed on the basis of the danger potential of the substance, its behaviour on the various exposure pathways and the expected exposure of the various receptors to be protected. Hazard assessments should take into account the current and future use of the groundwater.

To determine whether or not a hazard is present, one should show that a receptor has already been affected or that the probability of adverse impact within the foreseeable future is sufficiently great.

Formalized assessment models that take into account the criteria and/or parameters to characterize pollutants, sites and uses within surrounding areas are considered very useful. However, the outcome of model calculations should always be verified by an assessment commission which should include representatives of all parties concerned. Each case should be assessed individually, since the local geological, physical and hydrological conditions have a decisive influence on the need for treatment and on its extent.

Data collection and monitoring programmes should be tailored to the required information level, which is determined by the assessment goal (e.g. initial assessment, comparative assessment, detailed assessment). These programmes should use standardized sampling and laboratory procedures.

It would not be appropriate to set standards or quality classes to be achieved in groundwaters, because of the different natural conditions, human impact, and water uses that exist and the fact that many of the processes involved in the movement and breakdown of substances in the soil and in groundwater are not yet fully understood.

Therefore, a non-binding value system should be drawn up to help assess the degree of pollution and evaluate pollution loads. The system should not be applied schematically. It should include:

(a) Reference values which specify the natural background quality;

(b) Test values which represent warning levels. If they are not reached, no further measures are needed;

(c) Threshold values which represent action levels. As a rule, if these values are exceeded, further measures such as abatement, containment or rehabilitation should be undertaken to eliminate risks to goods and resources to be protected.

Goals for cleaning up contaminated sites range from mere hazard prevention required by regulations to the ecologically desirable restoration of the *status quo ante* or of an area's multi-functionality. The minimum goals should be to:

(*a*) Prevent health hazards wherever possible;

(*b*) Prevent strong ecotoxicological effects and other significant adverse effects on the environment;

(*c*) Restore the potential for different uses of water resources.

Remediation technology

Restoration measures should be selected according to the type of pollutants involved and the characteristics of the aquifer concerned. Particular attention should be given to soil pollution from substances that can move easily through groundwater. The affected soils should be cleaned up immediately to prevent further propagation within the subsoil and within the aquifer. This will reduce the costs of aquifer restoration in the long term.

Consideration should be given to a combination of different available techniques for containment and clean-up, bearing in mind that active groundwater containment techniques are generally less difficult to set up than passive containment techniques, that the operation and maintenance of the former may be expensive, and that these methods have a different impact on the environment.

Mechanical waste-water treatment methods, such as settling and filtration, do not help to remove most pollutants from aquifers. Depending on local conditions, on-site treatment methods should include the use of aeration, ozone, activated carbon or bacteria, or a combination of these.

As they seem promising, *in situ* clean-up technologies should be further investigated and developed.

Liability

Groundwater and soil pollution should be prohibited in order to safeguard groundwater for the future. Legal action should be taken against those known to, or believed to, have violated soil or groundwater pollution regulations.

Strict liability for remedial action and compensation for damage should be introduced at the earliest possible stage.

Where appropriate, property owners or occupiers should bear secondary liability for remedial action and compensation for damage.

The authority of municipalities should be strengthened so that they can enforce restoration. This may require additional financial support.

The polluter-pays principle should also be applied to past pollution, according to regulations in force when the pollution occurred.

To speed up remedial action of highly prioritized old contaminated sites, the polluter-pays principle should, however, be applied in a flexible way, particularly in the following cases:

(*a*) The polluter has proved that action has been taken in good faith and in accordance with previous legislation; and/or

(*b*) The present property owner or occupier has proved that the property has been received in good faith without knowledge of the existence of polluting substances.

The party responsible for corrective action should be forced to act and compensate for damage. If the responsible party is unable to do so, secondary compensation in the form of a fund, an insurance or other financial instruments should be provided to cover the costs.

National and multinational military forces should be placed on the same footing as any other polluter.

Part Three

GUIDELINES ON LICENSING WASTE-WATER DISCHARGES FROM POINT SOURCES INTO TRANSBOUNDARY WATERS

as prepared by the task force on water pollution control from point sources, with France as lead country, and adopted by the Committee on Environmental Policy at its third session in May 1996

INTRODUCTION

The *Convention on the Protection and Use of Transboundary Watercourses and International Lakes* (Helsinki, 1992), hereinafter referred to as the Convention, imposes obligations on Parties to protect transboundary waters, *inter alia*, against pollution from point sources through the prior licensing of waste-water discharges, the application of the best available technologies for the treatment of industrial waste water containing hazardous substances, the use of at least biological treatment or equivalent processes for the treatment of municipal waste water, and the provision of information to the public on permits issued. The Convention also points to some specific cases where stricter requirements apply, which go beyond the obligation to use, for example, best available technology.[6]

With a view to providing guidance to countries when implementing the Convention and achieving a high level of protection of fresh water, ECE Governments should at least apply the following recommendations when considering granting permits for waste-water discharges from point sources located in catchment areas of transboundary waters which are likely to cause a transboundary impact, and when checking whether or not operators of installations comply with permit conditions.

These Guidelines draw on the experience of environmental and water experts designated by ECE Governments for the task force on the control of water pollution from point sources.[7] They also build upon the report on the prevention, control and reduction of water pollution from point sources: experience and problems in ECE countries.[8]

I. GENERAL RECOMMENDATIONS

Water management plans, water-quality objectives and action programmes to cut pollution are tools to guide the licensing process at the national level and for transboundary catchment areas. Generally, the procedures for drawing up these instruments should be consistent with the ECE *Guidelines on the ecosystem approach in water management*[9] and the Recommendations to ECE Governments on water-quality criteria and objectives.[10]

Experience has shown, however, that efforts to develop jointly a common long-term strategy (e.g. a joint water management plan) for transboundary catchment areas among two or more countries riparian to the same transboundary waters may be time-consuming. For the purpose of licensing waste-water discharges into transboundary waters, it is therefore strongly recommended to start drawing up and implementing joint water-quality objectives and action programmes rather than immediately developing joint water management plans.

Licensing waste-water discharges and water management plans

Water management plans should consolidate requirements for the protection of water bodies and requirements for the actual and potential (future) uses of these waters. They should also define concepts regarding the conservation of water bodies and methods to improve or

---

[6] Convention on the Protection and Use of Transboundary Watercourses and International Lakes done at Helsinki, on 17 March 1992. E/ECE/1267. Geneva, 1992.

[7] The task force on the control of water pollution from point sources was led by France. The task force was composed of experts designated by the Governments of Croatia, the Czech Republic, Finland, France, Germany, Hungary, Poland, Slovakia and Slovenia. The ECE secretariat assisted the task force to draw up the Guidelines.

[8] The updated version (30 April 1996) of this report is part of document ECE/CEP/31.

[9] See footnote 4, p. 9.

[10] Recommendations to ECE Governments on water-quality criteria and objectives. In: *Water Series No. 2—Protection and Sustainable Use of Waters—Recommendations to ECE Governments*. ECE/CEP/10. United Nations. New York and Geneva, 1995.

restore their quality by systematically resolving problems encountered in the light of established priorities. The water management plans also set out recommendations addressed to the different levels of government authority, including local governments, to resolve these problems.

Usually, water management plans are not legally binding. However, it is expected that they will guide decision-making regarding physical planning and licensing and other procedures.

Clear commitments by the governments of the riparian countries and environmental objectives set in the context of a broad cooperative approach, are a fundamental prerequisite for a successful long-term water management policy. As a strategic framework, water management plans should be directed towards a level of decision-making which can really modify physical planning and any significant polluting activity in the catchment area.

Water management plans should be drawn up at different levels depending on the distribution of competencies between national authorities. Plans drawn up at the local level should be used to support the drafting of water-quality objectives and action programmes for the whole transboundary catchment area or parts thereof and vice versa. Independent experts may be involved in such issues as the study and validation of basic ecological data, modelling of water systems, risk and hazard assessment and conflict analysis. Representatives of the operators of installations, both in the industrial and in the municipal sectors, should participate in the assessments of the current situation, and be consulted on the forecasts of structural, technological and economic development in their respective sectors and on the impact of emission targets on technology.

The involvement of all parties concerned (e.g. managers, planners, policy makers at the appropriate levels of government and representatives of major groups) and the utilization of technical know-how and research results, are vital if a water management plan is to be accepted and successfully implemented. Particular care should be given to the thorough assessment of the initial situation in the catchment area (i.e. the present status of waters, including data on water quality and quantity, causes of pollution and identification of emissions) and its links with the economic development in the area. Another critical issue is the forecast of economic development within the area and the assessment of trends in pollution sources and the volume and composition of waste waters within the catchment area.

Assessment of the current situation

Assessments of the current situation should cover as a minimum:

(a) Assessment of the current physical, chemical and biological quality of surface waters and their sediments, and groundwaters, including an evaluation of trends and a comparison with quality standards for receiving water bodies stemming from the legislation in force. Usually, the existing monitoring network can be used. In some cases, tailor-made monitoring systems may be necessary. Geographical information systems (GIS) are frequently used for processing information and presenting it in map form;

(b) Recording of quantitative data, taking into account, *inter alia*, ecologically acceptable minimum flow rates, ecomorphological aspects, and the variability of the water flow;

(c) The total input of the pollution load into the water bodies in the catchment area.

An inventory of pollution sources should be drawn up. The information required for the inventory should be gathered in close cooperation with the operators of the installations concerned.

The inventory of pollution sources should provide information on the location of those point sources of pollution in the given catchment area that may have a transboundary impact.[11] Moreover, the inventory should contain a description of production activity, the characteristics of discharged pollution and quantitative data on the individual components in the waste water (concentration and load per unit of time). The inventory should also specify existing waste-water treatment facilities (their efficiency, design capacity and capacity utilization) and include an evaluation of their efficiency and a comparison with the best available technology (BAT); it should also contain information on expected changes and developments.

Water quality objectives, targets to reduce the pollution load and priority-setting

Water-quality objectives are regarded as a policy goal to be attained within a certain period of time. Catchment planning (territorial development plans) together with national environmental policy as regards water should be at the root of water-quality objectives. Catchment planning should also provide the context in which demand from all water users can be balanced against water quality requirements. Moreover, it should be shown for each transboundary catchment area or its relevant parts that national and international requirements regarding pollution reduction are properly taken into account in the planning process.

Account should be taken of the fact that the setting of water-quality objectives is a political process which involves decisions on the use of the water body concerned, careful assessments of economic conditions and present and future water uses, forecasts regarding industrialization and the consideration of many other socio-economic

---

[11] According to the Convention, transboundary impact means any significant adverse effect on the environment resulting from a change in the conditions of transboundary waters caused by a human activity, the physical origin of which is situated wholly or in part within an area under the jurisdiction of a Party, within an area under the jurisdiction of another Party. Such effects on the environment include effects on human health and safety, flora, fauna, soil, air, water, climate, landscape and historical monuments or other physical structures or the interaction among these factors; they also include effects on the cultural heritage or socio-economic conditions resulting from alterations to those factors.

factors. In this process, special attention should also be given to the protection of biodiversity and the safeguarding of the ecological potentials.[12,13]

Experience shows that, if not set with sufficient care, pollution reduction targets for point sources may affect the credibility of the environmental authorities. For point sources, it is therefore recommended that:

(a) The state of the industrial plants and activities that use or generate hazardous substances, and of the related transport and storage facilities, should be assessed before any targets are set;

(b) Reduction targets should be understandable to all parties involved and convertible into operational and cost-effective measures;

(c) It should be possible to monitor compliance with such targets. Targets that are either vague or too sophisticated should be avoided;

(d) Targets should be guiding, not normative, as the final emission limits are laid down in the licence;

(e) Reduction targets should have realistic time schedules; long-term targets can be set, showing the ultimate goal;

(f) The setting of priorities for the control of water pollution from point sources (e.g. categories of substances to be considered, discharges) should take place at the catchment level.

To set priorities so as to reduce pollution loads from those sources with the highest adverse impact on water quality first, the following actions are recommended: define the key negative factors and rank them according to their relative importance; list the requirements for water quality and quantity and/or protection and improvement of the environment most affected by these negative influences; evaluate the urgency of measures to be taken; estimate their economic feasibility on the basis of the results of environmental impact assessments, in order to formulate recommendations for priorities; and make adjustments in the public interest.

It is also expected that action programmes with timescales will be drawn up to specify the concrete tasks to be carried out to attain the general objectives set out in the water management plan. The conditions for, and costs of, implementing the measures set out in water management plans are also expected to be further specified within the action programmes. Moreover, the action programmes should cover follow-up to the implementation of projects.

The control of point source emissions in a transboundary catchment area may be supported by a number of policy instruments and be subject to limitations and specific requirements, such as nature conservation, limitations on the exploitation of river banks or shorelines, environmentally sound infrastructure projects, water use restrictions, the outcome of impact assessments in a transboundary context, public inquiries and other consultations when granting permits. Therefore, an essential goal of, first, water-quality objectives and action programmes and, then, water management plans is to provide a set of proposals for high-level decisions by riparian countries and/or proposals for drawing up appropriate bilateral or multilateral agreements.

The process of drawing up such instruments (water-quality objectives, action programmes and water management plans) has to be backed by all parties concerned. Moreover, the planning process should be approved and co-financed, if need be, by the governments of the riparian States and be coordinated by a joint body.

In addition to specific provisions of the Convention related to public information, the general public should also be well informed about the planning process and decisions taken on reduction targets and priorities of action in a transboundary catchment area. The implementation of water-quality objectives, action programmes and water management plans—possibly through an international agreement—usually remains the duty of authorities in the countries concerned, rather than that of the joint body.

Research, training and the exchange of information are needed to help decision makers to set reasonable priorities. Roles and responsibilities in water management should be clearly defined at the national, provincial and local levels, and cooperation between local authorities should be strengthened. This will also improve transboundary cooperation.

II. LICENSING WASTE-WATER DISCHARGES

Licensing waste-water discharges into rivers and lakes, and—if not prohibited by national law—into groundwaters, is a basic tool to ensure the protection, conservation and restoration of waters, with regard to both quality and quantity, and related ecosystems including aquatic flora and fauna. The integrated cross-media approach, which is being developed in various countries and international forums, should be further promoted.

Obligations set out in the Convention, supranational law, international agreements and national legislation on the protection and use of waters, for example, prohibiting emissions or setting emission limits for hazardous substances, lay down minimum requirements to be complied with for any permit to be granted. The emission limit values and equivalent parameters and technical measures should be based on BAT without prescribing the use of any technique or specific technology. However, the technical characteristics of the installation concerned and environmental conditions should be taken into account. In all circumstances, the condition of the permit should contain provisions on the minimization of

---

[12] See footnote 10, p. 31.

[13] Guidelines for developing water-quality objectives and criteria. In: *Annex III to the Convention on the Protection and Use of Transboundary Watercourses and International Lakes done at Helsinki, on 17 March 1992.* E/ECE/1267. Geneva, 1992.

long-distance or transboundary pollution and ensure a high level of protection of the environment as a whole. Exceptions can be made for small emission sources provided that these are not likely to have a transboundary impact.

A sound licensing system should preferably be based on case-by-case consideration of emission sources and on the outcome of impact assessments. This is because the characteristics and the capacity of watercourses vary with such factors as the geology, geomorphology and other features which determine the hydrological regime. Moreover, quality objectives set for a catchment area depend on the needs of current and future water users and the requirements for the protection and conservation of water bodies.

To establish limit values for both pollution concentration and load, it can be helpful to use mathematical models designed to assess the impacts from one or more point sources on waters and to predict the effects of, or to choose between, alternative options for setting permit conditions.

Some of the above-mentioned legal instruments applicable to licensing result in limit values for discharges being expressed solely in terms of concentration values. However, the setting of compulsory limit values which consider only the concentration of substances in effluents may give rise to an increase in the use of water to dilute waste waters or to the mixing of waste water from different production processes of the same enterprise which could be more efficiently treated separately. Therefore, limit values for the total discharge per polluting substance—expressed, for example, in mass units per time period—also have to be laid down in the permits.

In cases where stricter requirements than those related to the use of BAT apply, limit values for the discharge of polluting substances should be assessed case by case in the light of the requirements for the protection of aquatic ecosystems and to guarantee that needs are met for the most demanding water uses, for example, the supply of drinking-water. Special attention must be given to hazardous substances and nutrients. This is of major importance for watercourses that flow into lakes, for waters that suffer from eutrophication, and for waters which are prone to sedimentation and the subsequent release of hazardous substances from the sediments. If the water-quality objectives of the receiving water body cannot be met, additional measures exceeding BAT are required which may include restrictions or even a ban on the production and/or application of the mentioned hazardous substances and nutrients.

Compliance with quality objectives drawn up with due consideration of future economic development is only one objective of the licensing process. The conservation and, where possible, the restoration of aquatic ecosystems to a target state of high ecological quality— one of the major goals of water management policy— should become a guiding principle in the granting of permits. The minimization of emissions at the process level—a characteristic of the best available technology—is another requirement to be taken into account in the licensing process. This includes the control of pollutants within industrial processes, the saving of raw materials, the selective treatment of industrial waste water allowing the recycling of water, and the recovery of valuable substances, where appropriate. The appropriate measures also include totally or partially prohibiting the production or use of hazardous substances. The use of less hazardous substitutes for potentially hazardous substances in industry, trade and services may be contemplated.

Licensing waste-water discharges is a cumbersome and time-consuming task for the competent authorities. It requires well-organized staff with competence in legal, technical and ecological matters in order to grant or refuse permits within a reasonable period of time, and to review granted permits at regular intervals. Particularly in countries in transition, special attention should be given to the human resources development and institutional capacity building.

Usually, the authorities have to cope with a large number of permit applications for small and medium-sized installations rather than applications for major installations. Simplified procedures have therefore been drawn up in some countries to authorize discharges from installations which would not have a significant impact on receiving waters. However, a decision on whether or not to follow a simplified procedure cannot be left to the discretion of the local authorities, which are usually in charge of granting permits. This practice has to be regulated at the national level. Such regulations stipulate, for example, that limit values for small discharges are based on normative prescriptions.

The decision to grant or refuse a permit for waste-water discharge requires adequate information on the characteristics of the installation, which must be provided by the operator. The drawing-up of a set of minimum information requirements to be sought from the applicant is an urgent task, in particular where the installation has potential impacts on transboundary waters.

At the very least, information on the production or activity and the possible sources of emissions from installations should be provided. This would include information on the quantity and quality of emissions, the proposed measures to prevent the discharge of pollutants from the installation, proposed treatment measures and the expected discharges. Moreover, an assessment of whether or not a transboundary impact is likely to occur should become an integral part of permit applications. Furthermore, an outline of proposed measures for the prevention of, preparedness for, and response to industrial accidents should become part of the permit application. A precise description of proposed measures and practices to monitor emissions into receiving environments and sewer systems should also appear in the permit application. Recent experience has also demonstrated the need to provide information on proposed measures to be taken in the event of a complete cessation of the operation of the installation, to ensure that no impact on waters occurs.

The licensing procedure should be impartial vis-à-vis the rights and interests of the applicant and transparent to any parties, including the public, that have an interest in the protection and use of the waters in question. This would make it necessary, inter alia:

(a) To take advice from independent experts on environmental protection and public health issues;

(b) To consult local authorities in whose jurisdiction significant impacts from the proposed activity may occur;

(c) To conduct a public inquiry in the area subject to significant impacts.

Moreover, the applicant should have the right of reply to the outcome of these procedures.

After a period of time, the competent authority must consider the need to revise the prescriptions in the permit, or even to cancel it. To this end it must be able to draw on a very clear set of criteria drawn up for the purpose.

Usually, the procedures for the revision of permit conditions are similar to the procedures for granting the initial permit. A public inquiry or hearing may, however, not be required if the environmental impact of the activity under revision is unlikely to be significant.

Any licensing provisions would be ineffective if not accompanied by supervision and sanctions for non-compliance. Compliance monitoring is the responsibility of the competent national authorities. Penal sanctions are usually decided upon by the courts of justice or similar authorities.

There are several approaches to choosing an appropriate institutional framework for the management of transboundary waters, including the granting or refusal of permits. The possible solutions depend, *inter alia*, on:

(a) Whether the water body forms or crosses the border;

(b) The character of the water body;

(c) The degree and character of its use;

(d) The experience gained from earlier cooperation.

They also depend on whether or not the agreement in question contains specific obligations for the licensing, supervision and monitoring of pollution sources.

For licensing, an agreed notification system together with an agreed procedure for impact assessments of the pollution arising from point sources seem to be a minimum requirement for cooperation on transboundary waters. The joint body established by riparian countries should supervise the cross-border notification system.

To improve cooperation in the licensing of discharges of waste waters, some other issues may be of special interest, if not already regulated by applicable international law:

(a) Where a country is aware that the operation of an installation is likely to have a significant adverse impact on the environment of another country, or where a country likely to be significantly affected so requests, the country where the application for the permit was submitted should forward the information provided to the other country at the same time as it makes it available to its own nationals. Such information should serve as a basis for any consultation necessary in the framework of bilateral/multilateral relations between the countries concerned on a reciprocal and equal basis;

(b) Within the framework of bilateral/multilateral relations, the public of the country likely to be affected should have the right to comment on permits before the competent authority takes a decision;

(c) If one of the parties so requests, the prescriptions proposed for a permit for discharges likely to cause significant transboundary impacts should be examined by an independent institution, within a limited period of time, before a decision is taken by the authority in the upstream country. Any recommendation made by this body should be duly taken into account when negotiating a compromise solution for the prescriptions of the permit itself, and/or when deciding on remedial measures and compensation for damage, if applicable. A procedure should also be established which gives major groups of a downstream country the possibility to appeal against the decisions taken by an upstream licensing authority;

(d) When emissions from a point source do not seem to cause significant downstream impact, the competent national authority in the upstream country could inform the other party of permits granted, without prior consultation.

III. MONITORING OF POINT POLLUTION SOURCES AND SUPERVISION

All waste-water discharges from point sources which may have a transboundary impact should be monitored. In setting up and operating such monitoring systems, the methodology outlined in the Guidelines on water-quality monitoring and assessment of transboundary rivers[14] should be applied. Specific criteria and/or factors to be taken into account when assessing the significance of an impact and determining the content of monitoring programmes include the volume of waste water produced per time unit, the composition of the waste water, discharge patterns, and the characteristics of the receiving water bodies.

As monitoring of emission sources should provide information to help assess the potential hazards posed by point sources to the environment, it is important to obtain data on pollution loads rather than solely concentrations of pollutants.

Self-monitoring should be an integral part of the monitoring of point sources. This should include measurements of characteristics of side streams before treatment and the characteristics of the final waste water before discharge. Conditions and requirements for self-monitoring, such as parameters to be analysed, the frequency of measurements, quality assurance of data and the frequency and form of reporting to authorities, should be laid down in conjunction with the permit. Procedures should accordingly be established to that effect.

---

[14] Guidelines on water-quality monitoring and assessment of transboundary rivers. See part one above.

These procedures should also require—as further developed in the Guidelines on water-quality monitoring and assessment of transboundary rivers—that physico-chemical and biological tests of waste waters carried out by the operator of an installation or by a third party are certified and/or supervised by an independent, accredited laboratory which complies with international standards.

The programmes for monitoring waste-water discharges from point sources into transboundary waters should be designed and revised, if need be, to provide information which is necessary to assess whether or not the emissions have a significant adverse transboundary impact on human health and safety, flora, fauna, soil, air, water, climate, landscape and physical structures.

Monitoring the performance of production or processing operations should be part of pollution load supervision. Inspectors should have the right to enter facilities and check the pollution loads of the side streams and indoor streams and the waste water discharged into recipient water bodies. The specific pollution load per unit mass or volume of product or used raw materials and additives should be subject to monitoring and inspection as this helps to assess the environmental behaviour of the operator. The efficiency of waste-water treatment facilities should also be checked.

Operators of installations should provide all necessary assistance to the inspectors to enable them to carry out appropriate inspections, to take samples and to gather any other information required to check compliance with permit conditions.

Mechanisms should be set up to ensure that transboundary impacts are detected and reported without delay.

Joint supervision of point sources by the authorities of riparian countries may be necessary for installations that constitute a potential hazard to transboundary waters. Joint bodies could decide on criteria for the case-by-case selection of point sources that would be jointly supervised.

A comprehensive and systematic exchange of information between the riparian countries is a basic requirement of joint measures to prevent, control and reduce transboundary pollution from point sources. It should become an ongoing task of the competent national authorities of the riparian countries. If not classified as confidential, self-monitoring data should be included in the common programme of information exchange. To be effective, the exchange of such information should be governed by rules jointly agreed by the parties, specifying the format and frequency of reporting. The creation and maintenance of a joint database could also be useful.

IV. ECONOMIC INSTRUMENTS

Economic instruments should encourage operators of installations to apply best available technology. They should be considered as a supplement to direct regulations and administrative procedures for the control of water pollution from point sources. They should also motivate polluters to introduce pollution control measures voluntarily.

Economic instruments should be consistent with the polluter-pays principle. The most important instrument for the control of discharges from point sources is therefore a charge on activities that generate pollution, such as waste-water discharges. The efficiency of a charge system depends on the encouragement of the polluter to take pollution control measures in order to save money, rather than pay the charge.

Therefore, emission charges should reflect the potential harmfulness and volume of the pollutants discharged. Charges based on normative values of quantities of pollutant emissions from the production process or the activity prior to any waste-water treatment may also be used, combined with rebates for the abatement of discharges.

These charges should be high enough to provide a strong impetus to control and reduce waste-water discharges through appropriate in-process and/or waste-water treatment technology. Charges with little incentive impact may have negative effects on the polluter's behaviour. However, the actual amount of a charge should be tailored to the national situation, particularly in the countries in transition, and should be increased gradually to tackle the most severe environmental impacts first.

The revenue from such charges should be used for environmentally sound purposes. In many countries, the revenue or at least part of it is paid into a fund to promote pollution control measures.

V. CONSEQUENCES OF VIOLATION

There should be fines and sanctions for violating pollution control regulations. They should depend on the extent to which established limits, standards or norms are exceeded.

Fines and sanctions should be high enough to prompt compliance and compensate for damage. However, they should be based on a case-by-case examination of the infringement of legal and regulatory provisions.

There should be compensation for damage in addition to administrative and penal sanctions. Claims for compensation could be included in administrative or penal proceedings; however, they depend on private law.

Economic benefits arising from the infringement of regulatory prescriptions should be confiscated.